Aiden F.

A practical guide to
Tropical Aquarium Fish

Siamese fighting fish
(Betta splendens)

A practical guide to
Tropical Aquarium Fish

Richard Crow and Dave Keeley

Wimplefish (Heniochus acuminatus)

CLB

HOW TO USE THIS BOOK

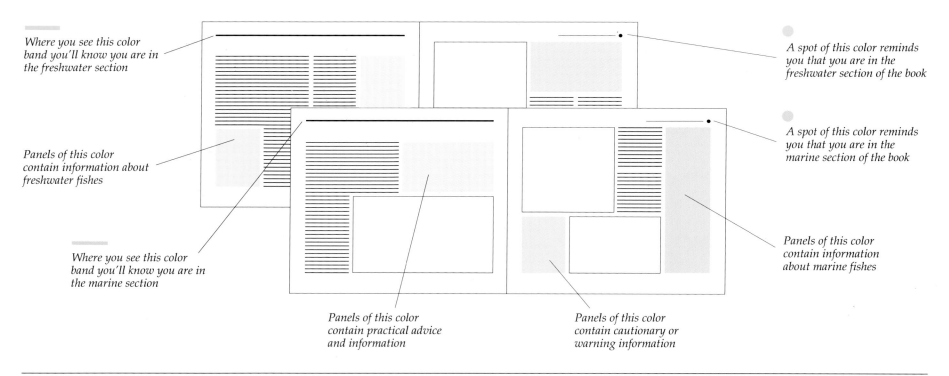

Where you see this color band you'll know you are in the freshwater section

Panels of this color contain information about freshwater fishes

Where you see this color band you'll know you are in the marine section

A spot of this color reminds you that you are in the freshwater section of the book

A spot of this color reminds you that you are in the marine section of the book

Panels of this color contain information about marine fishes

Panels of this color contain practical advice and information

Panels of this color contain cautionary or warning information

2911 Tropical Aquarium Fish
This edition published in 1999 by CLB
an imprint of Quadrillion Publishing Ltd
Godalming, Surrey, GU7 1XW, UK

Distributed in the USA by
Quadrillion Publishing, Inc.
230 Fifth Avenue, New York 10001

ISBN 1-84100-242-9
Printed in Hong Kong

Credits
Edited and designed: Ideas into Print
Photographs: Neil Sutherland
Typesetting: Ideas into Print and
Bureau 2000
Commissioning Editor: Andrew Preston
Production: Ruth Arthur,
Sally Connolly, Andrew Whitelaw
Director of Production: Gerald Hughes

THE AUTHORS

Richard Crow began keeping tropical fish in 1971, and following initial success with breeding livebearers, he moved on to keeping larger and more unusual species. Having successfully bred cichlids, particularly Central American cichlids, he began to specialize in this area and created a purpose-built fish house for breeding cichlids, home at one point to over 3,000 young and 17 breeding pairs. From 1985 until 1988 Richard was editor of the British Cichlid Association's two main publications. He has contributed to one previous book and has written countless articles for publications in the United Kingdom and overseas.

Dave Keeley has been an aquarist for over 25 years. Marine fish are his true interest - he has kept them since 1973 - and he is fascinated by the continuing development of the hobby. His professional interest in fishkeeping began in 1971 and today he is Managing Director of his own company, importing and distributing specialist aquatic equipment, particularly for marine aquariums, from the USA and Europe. This is Dave's second book and he regularly contributes to British and American fishkeeping journals, as well as lecturing on marine fish at clubs and shows throughout the United Kingdom.

PHOTOGRAPHER

Neil Sutherland has more than 25 years experience in a wide range of photographic fields, including still-life, portraiture, reportage, natural history, cookery, landscape and travel. His work has been published in countless books and magazines throughout the world.

FRESHWATER CONSULTANT

Gina Sandford has kept and bred many species of tropical fish, but catfishes are her special interest. She writes for fishkeeping journals, gives lectures and audio-visual presentations and is currently Secretary and Editor for the Catfish Association of Great Britain.

CONTENTS

FRESHWATER SECTION

Tropical fresh waters vary enormously around the world, from the dark, soft, acidic waters of rivers flowing through South America to the crystal-clear, hard and alkaline waters of the African Rift Valley Lakes. All abound in fascinating fishes that can grace the home aquarium.

CREATING YOUR OWN FRESHWATER AQUARIUM

FRESHWATER FISHES FOR YOUR AQUARIUM

MARINE SECTION

Although the salinity of sea water varies slightly around the tropical world, the marine environment is remarkable for its stability. This is the biggest challenge facing marine fishkeepers, but it is a challenge well worth accepting for the pleasure of keeping such stunningly beautiful fish.

CREATING YOUR OWN MARINE AQUARIUM

MARINE FISHES FOR YOUR AQUARIUM

Cosby blue gourami (Trichogaster trichopterus)

CREATING YOUR OWN FRESHWATER AQUARIUM

'We had a fish tank but all the fish died.' 'Our tank kept going green.' These comments are all too commonly heard among disillusioned, would-be fishkeepers, which is a shame, because fish need not die and tanks need not go green if they are set up and maintained correctly. In this opening section of the book, we look at the practical aspects of setting up a basic freshwater tropical aquarium and answer many of the questions that arise in the process. Start by planning ahead, think about the type and size of aquarium you would prefer, enquire about the availability of equipment and investigate local aquarium dealers. Some time spent on these vital early stages will undoubtedly save you heartbreak and, indeed, money later on.

In the first section you will find practical advice on selecting a freshwater aquarium and installing the necessary filtration, lighting and heating equipment. Once these early stages are complete, you can begin to furnish and decorate the tank, before buying and introducing the fishes you wish to keep. Later sections deal with feeding and maintaining your stock, as well as coping with health problems and encouraging your fishes to breed.

One word of caution. Success is never instant, least of all in fishkeeping. Be sure to give your tank time to settle down before putting in the plants, and allow the filtration system to begin to function effectively before introducing the first few fishes. Soon you will enjoy the fascination of keeping a healthy, well-maintained tropical freshwater aquarium.

Setting up a freshwater aquarium

Estimating capacity in 'cubes'

A cube of water measuring 4in on each edge has a volume of about 0.27 gallon.

A tank measuring 24x12x12in has room for 6x3x3 of these 4in cubes.

That makes 54 cubes in all, so the tank will hold about 15 gallons.

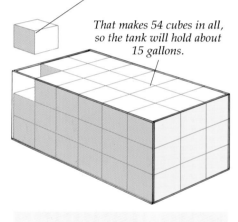

How to calculate the weight water in your aquarium when it is full

To calculate the weight of water in your aquarium, multiply the length, width and height of the aquarium in inches and divide the result by 230 to obtain the volume in gallons. Since water weighs about 8.3lb per gallon, you can calculate the weight of water in the full aquarium by multiplying the volume by 8.3.

Before considering the size of aquarium and where to put it in your room, you should first step outside the home and locate your nearest aquarium dealer.

Making contact with your local dealer

Once you have found your local aquarium shop, have a general browse around inside before buying equipment or deciding on anything for certain. Is the shop going to be able to supply the goods you need? Are the staff helpful? Most important of all, are all the tanks nicely presented and kept clean and tidy? Do the fish look healthy? If you peer into a tank and there are several dead fish in it or if several tanks have the odd dead fish, leave and take your custom elsewhere. Are there plenty of customers going in and out of the store? If so, this is usually a sign of a reputable shop. In most cases, it is better to go to a specialist aquarium dealer rather than a general pet shop. Although there are many pet shops that have good stocks of tropical fish and keep them in excellent condition, they are usually dealing in a wide range of animals and may not be able to give you the specialist help you need. Once you have located a dealer nearby and you've seen all those lovely exotic fish, you'll want to get started.

Where to put the aquarium?

The first thing to do is to decide where you want to put the tank. This decision requires some thought for several reasons. Firstly, the floor must be strong enough to stand the weight of the finished aquarium. Water weighs about 8.3lb per gallon, and as even a small aquarium suitable for a beginner holds about 15 gallons, this will weigh over 124lb as a minimum. Fortunately, the load of this weight will be spread over quite an area, so unless the floor is rotten or of dubious quality, you should have no problem, but it is wise to inspect it first. Bear in mind that first floors are usually stronger than upper floors, so pay particular attention if the tank is going upstairs. Wooden floors can be strengthened by nailing a layer of 0.5in-thick plywood over the area the tank will occupy.

Be sure to check if any sunlight falls where your tank will be situated. Excessive light will cause the growth of algae in your aquarium. Algae are primitive plant forms, and although not harmful - in fact, they provide a useful food source for many species of fishes - they can be unsightly if they get out of hand, so it is best to pick a spot where direct sunlight will not hit the tank. (See page 17 for advice on lighting the aquarium once you have set it up.)

Below: If you do decide to buy an all-glass tank, make sure that you place a layer of styrofoam about 0.5in thick under the base. The styrofoam will not collapse under the weight of the tank, but if there are any uneven places between the tank and the stand, the styrofoam will absorb them and prevent the bottom glass from cracking, which can have expensive consequences!

How much will standard size aquariums weigh?

Some popular sizes (LxWxD):

Size: 24x12x12in
Capacity: 15 gallons
Weight of water: 125lb

Size: 36x12x15in
Capacity: 28 gallons
Weight of water: 232lb

Size: 36x15x18in
Capacity: 42 gallons
Weight of water: 349lb

Size: 48x15x18in
Capacity: 56 gallons
Weight of water: 465lb

Next, decide what your aquarium is going to stand on. As mentioned earlier, water is heavy and with the added weight of gravel and rocks, a decorated aquarium will need a strong stand. Aquarium stands are available in many forms. Most aquarium shops sell very basic stands made of square steel framework, which are very safe and strong but quite basic in appearance, while some dealers can supply beautiful cabinets in virtually any wood finish and to any size. The choice of aquarium stands is unlimited. Some superb looking stands can be made from stone with built-in sections for books, video recorder, stereo units, etc. An aquarium can also make an excellent room divider where a room is so large that it needs something to break it into two.

It is advisable to place the tank in a warm (but not sunny) position if at all possible. Nobody wants to spend more money on the invisible commodity - electricity - than is necessary. The tank should also be placed where it can be seen and 'got at' without too much trouble. Try to pick a place where you can see it while you are sitting down in an armchair in the evening. Looking at the tank will become addictive and compulsive, and the last thing you want to do is contort yourself upside-down to see it. Try to make it a feature of the room rather than an afterthought.

Choosing your aquarium

Modern aquarium sealants can bond glass together with amazing strength. The basic aquarium is referred to as the 'all-glass' aquarium and that is virtually what it is; pieces of glass bonded together with sealant to form a container. All-glass aquariums are relatively inexpensive and perfect for keeping all sorts of fish. There are many shapes that can be made in this all-glass style: long and slim, tall and wide, multisided tanks in hexagons and octagons, or any shape you like. One type that is particularly popular is the large cube, which can be viewed from any of its four sides. You may prefer to have an aquarium with a frame so that the front of the tank looks like a picture. Framed tanks are available in many materials and colors but the frame is usually decorative rather than structural. Another design is the bow-fronted aquarium; this is made with a curved piece of toughened glass at the front to give a feeling of real depth. These tanks are attractive, but expensive.

The size of the aquarium is no problem at all. If you go to your local aquarium dealer they will be able to supply a tank made exactly to the size you require. Aquarium sealants are so good that it is not a problem to get them to cope with the water pressure, but finding a glass thick enough can be more difficult. Plastic tanks are available and quite inexpensive but their useful life is not as long as that of a glass tank due to the fact that plastic scratches easily and starts to look shoddy rather quickly.

Good aquarium sense

❏ A new aquarium should be tested and guaranteed, but it is wise to test it outdoors for your peace of mind. Simply fill it with water and check it for leaks.

❏ If you buy a secondhand tank and discover it has a leak, do not panic. You can use aquarium sealant to repair it. Find the spot that is leaking, clean and dry it thoroughly and apply a bead of sealant. This smells of vinegar, so carry out the job in a well-ventilated room. After the repair has set for 48 hours, your leaky tank will be good as new.

❏ Do not use sealants sold for bathroom and kitchen use. Although they look suitable they may contain fungicides, which are poisonous to fishes.

❏ Whatever type of tank you buy, never move it with water inside it as the varying pressures created by this can make it crack or spring a leak.

❏ Before you position the tank in your room, give it a good rinse with warm salty water. Do not use soap or detergent as they are poisonous to fishes.

Installing filters in your aquarium

All aquariums should have some form of filtration system to keep the water clean and healthy for the fishes. There are several types of filters and something to fit every need and every pocket.

Filters work in three ways: mechanical, chemical and biological. Basically speaking, a mechanical filter removes large particles suspended in the water, a chemical filter changes the chemical balance of the water, and a biological filter harnesses the cleansing power of colonies of bacteria to purify the water that flows through it. In practical terms, a simple biological filter performs all three types of filtration at the same time.

By far the best all-round biological filter is an undergravel filter. This usually consists of a corrugated piece of plastic with small holes or slots in it. In one corner there is a large round hole in which a plastic uplift tube fits. The whole thing is placed on the bottom of the tank and covered with a layer of gravel substrate to a depth of about 2-3in. When the tank is filled with water and an airline is placed down the uplift tube and connected to an air pump, the air bubbles rising to the surface in the tube draw water up with them and set up a flow of water down through the gravel layer over the entire base of the tank. In effect, the gravel acts like a tank-wide filter bed. Not only does this strain out suspended particles, but after a few hours, colonies of useful aerobic bacteria start to develop in the oxygen-rich conditions in the gravel, and over a period of weeks these will multiply and do battle with any harmful bacteria and chemical waste products. Instead of using rising air to power this type of filter system, a water pump can be fitted on the top of the uplift tube. This so-called 'power head' increases the flow rate through the filter bed and up to a point improves the efficiency of its filtration action. (This arrangement is featured in an illustration on page 86 in the section on marine aquariums.)

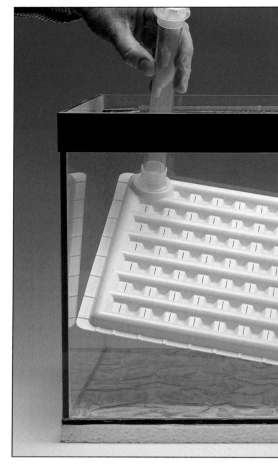

Below: This drawing shows how water circulates through an undergravel filtration system. The 'driving force' for the movement in this basic set-up is provided by air from an electric pump. The rising air bubbles in the uplift tube cause an upward flow of water that in turn 'pulls' water from underneath the filter plate across the whole base of the tank. As long as the pump is working the circulation continues. If you position the air pump as shown here it is advisable to fit a non-return valve in the airline to prevent water siphoning out of the tank if the pump stops.

How an undergravel filter works

Air supplied from an electric pump

Water is drawn down through the filter bed

Aerobic bacteria in the gravel break down ammonia wastes into less harmful nitrates

Rising air bubbles cause water to flow upwards

Water flows under filter plate towards uplift tube

How waste products are cycled

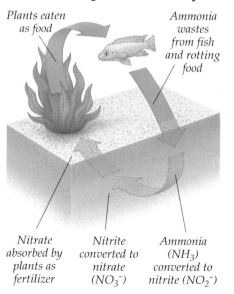

Plants eaten as food

Ammonia wastes from fish and rotting food

Nitrate absorbed by plants as fertilizer

Nitrite converted to nitrate (NO_3^-)

Ammonia (NH_3) converted to nitrite (NO_2^-)

Another type of filter is the external power filter. External power filters are usually canisters with an electrically driven water pump on top that draws water out of the tank, through the filter body and back into the tank. If the power filter is filled with coarse gravel, it will work in exactly the same way as the undergravel filter. Various alternative biological filter media are available; these are usually little ceramic rings or complicated plastic shapes with a large surface area for bacteria to grow on. External power filters are very versatile and when filled with a suitable medium, such as sponge or aquarium floss, they can also be used as mechanical filters. In fact, a good combination is to use an external power filter to mechanically clean up the water that flows through an undergravel filter in the tank. (This type of arrangement is particularly recommended for marine aquariums and is discussed on page 86.)

Other types of mechanical filter include simple power filters that fit inside the tank and air-powered box filters filled with aquarium floss that also go inside the aquarium. There are also sponge filters; these have their own air uplift and draw water through a cylinder of sponge. These give good mechanical filtration with quite a bit of biological action as bacteria grow within the sponge.

The air supply for filters comes from an air pump. These are obtainable from aquarium shops in a range of types and prices. Some make more noise than others and this may be an important consideration for a tank set up in the living room. Do not be tempted to use air pumps intended for anything other than aquariums; these pumps can have oils in them and if fish come in contact with oils of any type, they will die. Your aquarium dealer will be able to supply you with clear plastic tubing - universally called airline - which attaches to the pump and runs to the aquarium. The dealer will also supply valves, T-pieces and clamps so that you can run several airlines from one pump and adjust the air flow to various pieces of equipment as required. Make sure that your pump is placed above the water level so that if for any reason the pump should stop, water will not siphon back through it and onto the floor. If you cannot place the pump above the water level then fit a non-return valve in the airline near your pump. This will allow air to pass towards the tank but stops water flowing back.

An air supply is also needed in the tank in order to help the fish breathe. This is usually accomplished by passing air from the pump through an airstone that splits the air into masses of tiny bubbles. The rising column of bubbles moves the water around and, in doing so, helps it to absorb oxygen from the surface. There are many types and sizes of airstones; some are pieces of wood, others consist of sand particles glued together. Some dramatic effects can be created by positioning airstones so that they bubble up from under rocks or from underneath the layer of gravel on the base of the aquarium.

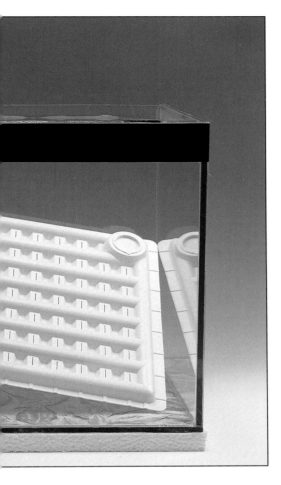

Above: Simply place the undergravel filter plate in the bottom of the bare tank as shown. These plates are available in standard sizes to fit a wide range of tanks. For larger tanks you can fit more than one filter plate as necessary, but do make sure that you insert an uplift tube into each plate. The best arrangement is to position the uplift tube in one of the rear corners, where it can be concealed by rockwork or plants. You can seal the sides of the plate to the tank glass with aquarium sealant to stop the water taking a 'short circuit' around the edge.

Above: Aquarium gravel is the best overall choice as a substrate. Before putting the gravel into the tank, wash it very thoroughly (without soap) until the water running away from it is clear.

Above: Cover the filter plate with a gravel layer about 2-3in deep. Avoid gravel used for building purposes as this may have stones which are not suitable for tank use. Sand is not ideal as the grains will clog together and stop water flowing through the plate. Pick a gravel with a particle size relevant to your fish, i.e. small gravel for small fish and larger gravel for larger fish.

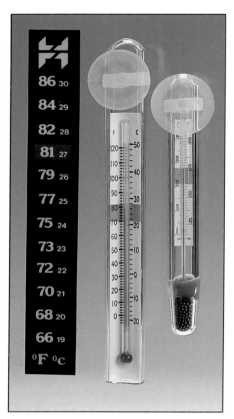

Heating the aquarium

The usual way of heating aquarium water is with one or more heater/thermostats. These are glass tubes with an electric element and thermostat inside them. On the top there is a small adjuster that usually turns by hand and controls the thermostat inside. When you buy a heater/thermostat they are usually set at 75°F, which is about the ideal all-round temperature. In fully submersible models the whole of the heater/thermostat goes in the tank and the wire comes out through the lid to be attached to an electricity supply. Heater/thermostats are available in various wattages, so you need to choose the right size for your aquarium. As a basic guide, allow 10 watts of heating for every gallon of water in the aquarium. Of course, during the summer months or if the tank is in a particularly warm spot you may not need as much heating capacity. You can install a higher wattage heater/thermostat to be on the safe side. These usually cost very little more to buy and indeed no more to run as they will burn more electricity while on but will be working for a shorter period. The only disadvantage of using a higher wattage heater/thermostat is that they are usually slightly larger than the next size down.

There are heater/thermostats available that have the adjuster built into the external lead, enabling you to adjust the temperature without getting your hands wet. Some models are fitted with microchips, and these types are highly accurate and hold the temperature steady within fine tolerances. There are heater elements that go underneath the gravel, but these are relatively expensive and have to be wired to a thermostat on the outside of the tank; nevertheless, they do mean that you have no problems trying to hide heater/thermostats behind rocks or plants. Under no circumstances should you ever put an ordinary glass tube heater/thermostat under the gravel as it will burn out, with disastrous effects. And no matter what type of heater/thermostat you use, always disconnect the electricity before adjusting the temperature control.

You need to install some method of keeping a check on the temperature of the water. There are various types of aquarium thermometers. Some float in the tank, others stick on the inside or outside of the glass. The most convenient type are the stick-on strip thermometers that change color according to the temperature of the water in the tank. These stick on the outside of the glass. The best configuration is to have the undergravel filter uplift and the heater/thermostat in one of the rear corners and the thermometer stuck on the outside of the glass at the opposite front corner. In this way, the water flow from the filter will carry the warm water from the heater/thermostat around the tank and the thermometer will be in what is most likely to be the coolest spot.

Above: There are several types of tank thermometers. The flat stick-on type at the extreme left is a good choice. Next to it are two spirit-filled models, the right hand one of which will also float. The one below has a movable pointer so that you indicate the desired temperature.

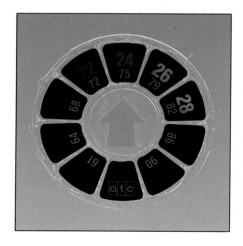

What total heater rating will my aquarium need?

Some popular sizes (LxWxD):

Size: 24x12x12in
Capacity: 15 gallons
Heater: 150 watts

Size: 36x12x15in
Capacity: 28 gallons
Heater: 250/300 watts

Size: 36x15x18in
Capacity: 42 gallons
Heater: 400 watts

Size: 48x15x18in
Capacity: 56 gallons
Heater: 550 watts

The above recommendations are based on allowing 10 watts of heating per gallon of water to maintain a temperature of 75°F in a normally heated room. Since aquarium heaters are usually rated in multiples of 50 watts, the closest appropriate rating has been suggested. Of course, you can fit two or more aquarium heaters of lower ratings to make up the figure.

Lighting the aquarium

Assuming the aquarium is going to be covered with a hood, the most suitable method of lighting is with fluorescent tubes. Tubes suitable for aquariums are very much the same as household ones and are available in various sizes. Do not make the mistake of buying a fluorescent tube exactly the same length as the tank; always buy the next size down so that it will fit inside the hood. You can alter the appearance of the aquarium with various types of tubes, including ones that enhance the red colors in fish and plants, as well as 'cooler' daylight balanced tubes that give a more neutral light. In fact, you can mix tubes of different sorts to get the best of both worlds. Keep lighting well away from the water and always use waterproof endcaps on the tubes; water and electricity do not mix!

Above: Attach the heater/thermostat to the inside back panel of the aquarium as shown here. The unit should come ready supplied with a rubber or plastic sucker for this purpose. Fix it at an angle so that the thermostat part of the unit is above the heater element, which occupies the lower part of the glass tube. Make sure it is a fully submersible model before positioning it where it will be covered completely with water. This photograph also shows the air pump in place, with a length of plastic airline running into the uplift tube.

If the aquarium is not going to be covered with a hood then there are other possibilities. Spotlights mounted on the wall above the aquarium and allowed to play down on the tank at varying angles can make dramatic effects. Shadows cast by intense spotlights, such as those fitted with metal halide bulbs, make superb places for timid fish to hide in and also give the tank a dramatic appearance. The movement of the water surface also creates very effective rippling patterns on the gravel. Mercury vapor lamps are ideal for lighting an aquarium. These are very powerful bulbs that burn incredibly white and use very little electricity compared to their light output. These can be mounted from the wall or direct from the ceiling above the tank and make a superb display. Avoid using ultraviolet tubes for safety reasons; looking directly at them can cause eye damage.

There are no fixed limits to lighting levels, all you need is enough light to be able to see the fish, so if the tank is in a bright spot, there is no need to have a light. However, if you plan to grow plants in your aquarium you will need at least 4 watts of lighting per gallon for healthy growth. Leave the lights on for 12 hours a day to simulate tropical daylength. Use a time switch to turn them on and off; remember that both fish and plants need a dark rest period.

Below: This photo shows a close up the airline running from the air pump into the uplift tube of the undergravel filter. There is a non-return valve fitted in the airline that will allow air to pass into the tank but will prevent water passing back into the pump should it fail. Since the end of the airline is submerged below water, there is a natural tendency for a siphonic flow to start up that would eventually drain the tank down to the level of the tube opening. Another way of guarding against this happening is to position the air pump above the level of the water in the aquarium.

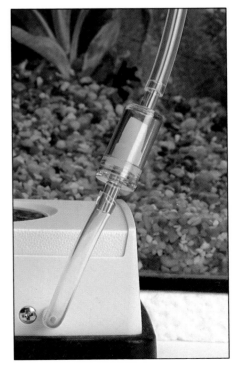

Completing the installation

The initial setting up is nearing completion now but there are a few loose ends to tie up. Firstly, there needs to be a cover glass; this glass or plastic cover goes over the top of the tank and stops any splashes coming into contact with the electricity and also stops fish jumping out - yes, they jump as well as swim! Whether you have a tank with a hood or not you still need a cover glass just to be safe. You can either buy a plastic cover glass from your dealer or get a piece of glass cut to size at a glass shop, but remember, if you do use glass, ask for each corner to be cut off to allow space for your wiring and airline to run through. Also have the edges smoothed to avoid damaging your hands on the glass as you maintain the aquarium. The next thing to do is to wire everything into the electricity. The heater/thermostat and air pump need to have electricity all the time, whereas the light needs a switch in the circuit so that you can turn it off during the night. The best thing to do is buy a switched connecting block called a cable tidy from your dealer. This will accommodate all the wires from your tank and allow you to use just one plug. A cable tidy has a switch for your light plus another spare switch and makes a good investment.

Having wired everything correctly and checked it all to make sure there are no water splashes on the electrics, plug in and switch on. With water and electricity so close together, it is vital to make sure that they do not come into contact with each other. Should this happen while you have your hands in the tank, you could suffer a nasty shock. A wise buy is a circuit breaker. This plugs into the mains and your plugs fit into it. Should a short circuit occur, the power to the tank is cut off in a fraction of a second before any ill-effect becomes apparent. Circuit breakers are not cheap pieces of equipment, but what price life?

Above: You can add rocks and other basic decorations before adding water to the tank. Make sure they are stable.

Guidelines for safe fishkeeping

❏ Water and electricity are dangerous if they come into contact. Disconnect the electricity before placing your hand in the tank and before adjusting or fitting electrical equipment.

❏ Always use the correctly rated fuse following the manufacturer's instructions and double insulate all electrical joints using proper electrical connectors.

❏ Make sure that any electrical equipment such as heater/thermostats are submersible before placing them in the water. Check your wiring regularly.

❏ Fit a cover glass over the water surface and make sure that any lighting cannot fall into the tank.

❏ Never set your tank up on an unsteady stand. If children are about, supervise them and never leave them alone with the tank.

❏ Aquarium remedies and medicines are a necessary part of the hobby. Do not put your hands in a tank that has any of these in it. Do not drink them and keep them out of the reach of children.

❏ Always read the instructions on any remedies and medicines and carry them out meticulously.

❏ Keep all fish foods out of the reach of children.

❏ A few fish are poisonous or electrically charged and these should be clearly labeled at the aquarium shop. Never place your hand in a tank with these fish. Avoid handling fish in general and never place your hand in an aquarium with piranhas or similar fishes. Remember that large catfishes, cichlids and some other fishes can bite, and may give you a nasty nip, especially if they mistake your finger for food.

Left: Ordinary tap water is fine for filling up the tank. Add enough hot and cold water so that when you put your hand in the tank it feels just cool but not cold. Trickle the water in slowly so that you do not disturb the gravel and any decorations already in the tank. In fact, directing the water onto a rock will reduce the impact of the flow. Continue adding water until the level is about 1in from the top of the tank.

Below: With the tank partially filled you can begin to put in the plants. Start with the back corners and progress forwards, leaving a central space for the fish to swim in. This plant has been raised in a plastic basket of rock wool medium. This simplifies planting and reduces the negative impact of the undergravel filter. Some plants featured in this photographic sequence are not true aquatic species and have been used for demonstration purposes only.

The basic aquarium kit

To set up a basic freshwater aquarium like the one featured on these pages you will need to buy the following items:

Stand
All-glass aquarium
Layer of styrofoam
Aquarium grade gravel
Undergravel filter (or some type of biological filter)
Air pump
Airstone
Airline, T-pieces and clamps
Heater/thermostat
Thermometer
Cable tidy
Cover glass
Light fitting
Rocks and plants

Above: Always fit a transparent cover on top of the aquarium, whether it is a custom-sized plastic one as shown here or a piece of glass cut to fit. If you are going to fit a hood with lights, then a cover will stop water splashing onto the electrical connections. A cover also prevents fishes jumping out. Keep the cover clean so that the maximum amount of light reaches the aquarium.

Right: Things are nearing completion now. This metal hood has space for one fluorescent tube, here wisely fitted with waterproof endcaps. The silvery finish inside the hood will help to reflect the maximum amount of light down into the aquarium. The black bulge on the lefthand side is a cable tidy - a plastic block that literally tidies up the wiring to the air pump, lights and filters.

Decorating your aquarium

Display aquariums are made or ruined by their decoration, so having looked briefly at a simple set-up now it's time to be at your most artistic and let your inspired talents flow!

Creating a suitable background

You can create a background from anything you choose or you can buy ready-made backgrounds from your dealer. These are usually long panoramic photographs of planted underwater scenes, which you can cut to length and apply to the outside back glass of your aquarium. Some dealers can supply three-dimensional backgrounds that make the tank look as if it has more depth of field. Plain-colored backgrounds are probably the most effective options. Blue and black are the most commonly used colors, but it is totally up to you - the fish will not mind what color the background is!

You can create a wide variety of background ideas. Crinkled up aluminum foil makes a good background applied to the outside, as do unvarnished cork tiles applied to the inside of the tank before adding the water. Why stick to one background? If you make a few for the outside of the back glass, you can have a swap around when the mood takes you. If you are successful with plants and the stand you have chosen has room, you can fill the background with lots of real plants and greenery. Set out carefully, they can blend in with aquatic plants inside the tank and create a superb effect.

Rocks in the aquarium

Most aquariums have rocks in them. Do take care, however, because not all rocks are suitable. The wisest option is to buy your rocks from an aquarium shop, but this can be expensive if you need a fair amount to create the right sort of underwater scene. Finding your own rock for the aquarium is more fun, plus the fact that it's nice to get something for nothing. As a general guide, if you come across rocks that have thin lines or veins of metal in

Below: You can create some dramatic effects by using dark, substantial rocks to form a fitting background for solid-looking fishes. Here a blue-eyed pleco (Panaque suttoni) *seems at home against a brooding aquascape of heavy granite pieces. You can indulge your full creative talents in building up a miniature scene within the aquarium. Make sure that you use rocks and other tank decorations that will not affect the water chemistry and thereby endanger your fishes, and anchor them securely so that boisterous fishes cannot rearrange your carefully worked-out scheme.*

Which rocks should I use?

Suitable rocks
The best rocks for most tanks are inert ones that do not affect the water chemistry, such as:

Granite
Basalt
Gneiss
Slate
Quartz

Unsuitable rocks
Avoid rocks with calcium and magnesium compounds that turn water hard and alkaline:

Limestone
Marble
Dolomite
Calcareous sandstones
Any soft, chalky rocks

Options for backgrounds

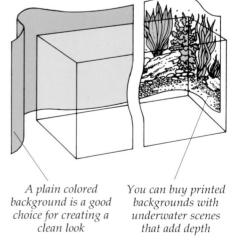

A plain colored background is a good choice for creating a clean look

You can buy printed backgrounds with underwater scenes that add depth

Above: This large piece of bogwood catches the light and provides an excellent focal point in the aquarium. You can also use vine roots - thinner and more textured than bogwood - to create interesting shapes and welcome crannies for the fish to swim in and out of. You can also use artificial versions.

Why not put some of your favorite houseplants behind the aquarium?

You can fix pieces of untreated cork bark inside the tank with aquarium sealant

them, leave them alone. Test any other rocks that you collect with a few drops of vinegar. If the vinegar fizzes vigorously then these rocks contain calcium compounds that will make the water harder and more alkaline and are suitable only for certain fishes. Do not worry too much if a few lines of little bubbles come up, as most rocks have some small calcium deposits. Soak rocks that have passed the acid test for a week in a bucket of water to remove the acid and leach out any other impurities. In fact, it is a good idea to thoroughly rinse rocks that you buy from your aquarium dealer.

Before placing rocks in the aquarium, slope the gravel from front to the back so that it is twice as deep at the back than at the front. This not only allows any debris to accumulate at the front, where it is easy to remove, but also provides a firmer foundation for embedding rocks and other tank decorations. When installing rocks, make sure that they cannot fall or subside. Place the largest, most stable rocks near the back corners to act as a base and then build on or around these. Try to create an overall view like a small stage in a theater, with an appropriate background, some props around the edges to give a three-dimensional feel and an open area in the middle for your 'cast' to act upon. Where possible, you can build the gravel up behind rocks and so vary the levels within the tank.

Remember that the rocks do not have to be laid horizontally; some great effects can be made by arranging several narrow pieces of slate vertically or even towering out of the tank. Using one type of rock has a superb effect or you can keep to one type in each particular part of the aquarium. Do not be afraid to use large pieces of rock; two large pieces always have a greater visual impact than four small pieces. If only small pieces are available, you can glue them together with aquarium sealant to make larger structures and even build up nice little walls by sticking tiny chips together.

The artistic possibilities of bogwood

Petrified wood, or bogwood, as it is called, makes a superb tank decoration. It usually comes from peat bogs and consists of tree roots that have been compressed over long periods of time. Bogwood is available from your dealer in various twisted shapes and sizes. To prepare it for the aquarium, soak it for a week in a bucket of water. Over this time, a dark residue will leach out and the water will begin to look like tea. After the week is up, remove the wood and let it dry. Once dried out completely, give it several coats of polyurethane varnish to stop further weeping of dyes. Wait another few days to make sure that the varnish is fully dry and then install it in the aquarium. As this wood is petrified, it usually sinks, but on occasions it may float. If this is the case, drill a couple of holes in a small piece of slate and screw it to the bottom of the bogwood to weigh it down. Use brass screws to avoid corrosion.

Other decorative materials

Cork
Cork looks very decorative in the aquarium. The only problem with cork is that it floats, so you need to devise some way of sinking it. The best method is to screw it to a piece of slate, as described for bogwood, or glue it to the aquarium glass with sealant before you fill the tank.

Bamboo
Bamboo canes placed vertically in the aquarium can make a very decorative display. To anchor the canes fit them into holes drilled into a piece of slate placed on the bottom of the aquarium. Do not worry if the canes do not fit tightly at first as they will swell when they have been in the tank for an hour.

Coal
Coal is totally safe in the aquarium and can provide a very decorative and inexpensive alternative to rockwork.

Flowerpots
Clay flowerpots - left whole or split in half - form excellent caves for fishes. Other builders' materials made from a similar red terracotta clay can be used to form caves or tunnels for fish. If you are not happy with the standard finish you can cover a clay pot with a thin layer of sealant and roll it in loose gravel to give it a coating that blends in superbly with the substrate.

Decorating with aquatic plants

Once you have installed the solid decorations, leave the aquarium undisturbed for a few days with the undergravel filtration system running. This period will allow the useful aerobic bacteria to develop in the gravel and the water to become clear. Keep an eye on the temperature and see that it does not fluctuate by more than a degree or two. Check that the light and pump are working well and that bubbles are flowing out of the uplift tube and from the airstone. After this period, you can start to introduce aquatic plants.

Plants can form a very attractive part of an aquarium but they are not essential for the fishes' health. The main reasons for having plants in the aquarium are that they will give the fish somewhere to hide and also supply the tank with oxygen. They will also compete for dissolved nutrients and hopefully get more than their fair share, thus leaving no food for unwelcome excess algae to live on. Reasons for not having plants in the tank are when the particular fishes you aim to keep are plant-eaters or gravel-diggers, or when your lighting levels are insufficient to support plant life.

Plants within the aquarium work in much the same way as those in pots around the house. Part of their daily process is to take in carbon dioxide and give off oxygen in return. As oxygen is used by the fish when they breathe and carbon dioxide is given off in return, it is easy to see that a sort of exchange process can be set up. There will never be an aquarium where the plants and fish give off enough gases for each other, but it is nice to think they are living in a harmonious relationship. The fish will also feed partly on the plant life, and their droppings will become a fertilizer for the plants, the plants returning the favor by breaking it down. Again, neither of these actions will be sufficient for the others' requirements but they are better than not being done at all. If plants are not present, the fish will not suffer; they will find other cover among the rocks and they will get oxygen from the work of the airstone and surface movement. So it's your choice, plants or no plants?

If you choose to have plants in the aquarium, there are other things to bear in mind. Firstly, plants will need fertilizers to keep them growing well, just as garden plants do. They will also need strong lighting if they are to flourish. You will need to remove any dying leaves trimmed in order to keep the tank looking at its best and prune any plants that outgrow their welcome.

Choosing and using real plants

The choice of real plants is enormous. Not only green, but also colored plants and flowering ones are available. Some only grow 1in high, others can reach as much as 24in. Some float on the surface, some nestle into little crevices. When you buy aquarium plants at your dealers, take a good look at them to see if they look healthy,

Below: The plants behind this clown loach (Botia macracantha) *are made of plastic. The tank has been set up for only a short time and so the plants still have that 'new' look, but after a few months the plastic fronds will become coated and will look surprisingly lifelike. There are plastic equivalents of a wide range of aquarium plants, from small foreground plants to tall ones with long fronds that are ideal for 'planting' along the back of the tank.*

Typical freshwater plants

Straight vallis
(Vallisneria spiralis)

Amazon sword
(Echinodorus paniculatus)

Hygrophila
(Hygrophila polysperma)

Dwarf anubias
(Anubias nana)

Red rotala
(Rotala macrarandra)

Water wisteria
(*Synnema triflorum*)

Green cabomba
(*Cabomba caroliniana*)

Water-worn
yellow sandstone

Dwarf fountain grass
(*Ophipogon japonicus var.*)

Corkscrew/twisted vallis
(*Vallisneria tortifolia*)

and avoid plants that have brown or yellowed leaves. The plants should be supplied to you in a plastic bag or styrofoam freezer-type pack. Try to keep them warm on their journey home, and when you remove the plants from their package try to avoid touching them as much as possible. If you do have to handle the plants, be as gentle as you can. Remove any dead or damaged leaves with a pair of scissors and then, holding the plant just above the roots, insert it into the gravel so that it just covers the lighter base of the plant, or crown. Do not push the plant in too far.

It is a good idea to add an aquarium fertilizer to the tank at this stage. Add this weekly or as the instructions recommend. You can also place fertilizer pellets in the gravel around the plants and these are excellent aids to their growth. Some plants are supplied in little perforated flowerpots. If this is the case, plant the whole pot under the gravel and cover the top of the pot with just a little gravel.

Why plants may not succeed

If you have trouble getting your plants to grow, there may be several reasons for this. Firstly, undergravel filters tend to play havoc with certain plants, causing them to die or grow in a strange manner. If you have used the undergravel method of filtration and experience problems with plants dying within days of buying them, it is likely to be the filter. You then have three choices: go for different plants, use a power filter with gravel in it for your biological filter, or revert to plastic plants. Another reason for plants dying is insufficient light. If you find your plants are dying gradually over the course of a few weeks, then this is probably the cause. Insufficient light is often associated with the growth of brown algae, which confirms that light is the problem. You can try fitting another fluorescent tube in the hood or use a bulb especially designed to boost plant growth.

Water conditions can be a further reason for plant failure. Some plants prefer soft water, whereas others like hard water. Most plants prefer alkaline rather than acid conditions, and if the temperature rises above 80°F, certain plants will start to die. Snails can also be harmful to plants. They will feed on decaying plants, but also on healthy plant material, just as snails do in the garden. And, of course, the fish themselves may attack your plants.

The benefits of plastic plants

If you are undecided, there is a genuine third choice between plants and no plants, and this choice is plastic plants. In the aquarium, they are often indistinguishable from the real thing and some even move in a realistic fashion. Plastic plants have the advantage that they do not die, do not overgrow the tank and last forever, literally. It really is worth considering plastic plants, especially if the only reason you cannot have plants is because your fish are plant-eaters.

Other aquatic plants

Fairy moss (*Azolla caroliniana*)
A very hardy floating plant with small rough leaves. There are several types, many of which vary in color; some change from green to red or purple.

Duckweed (*Lemna gibba*)
This consists simply of a very small floating leaf with a couple of roots. Provides shade and shelter for surface-dwelling fish. May block light to other plants.

**Water lettuce
(*Pistia stratiotes*)**
Like a floating lettuce up to 6in across. Long trailing roots hang down for fish to hide in.

**Hornwort
(*Ceratophyllum demersum*)**
Similar to cabomba, but with little rubbery leaves. Grows quickly and not bothered by undergravel filtration. Best planted in bunches at back of tank. Cuttings root easily.

**Hair grass
(*Eleocharis acicularis*)**
Literally a hairlike grass that grows to about 5in high. Looks best planted around rocks or pieces of bogwood.

Elodea
There are several types of this 'oxygenating weed'. It will grow rapidly in tropical aquariums as well as in coldwater tanks. Can float but best planted in gravel.

Buying and introducing your fish

By now your aquarium is all set up and running, with its rockwork and decor all laid out and any plants you have introduced are starting to become established. Once the undergravel filter has been running for a couple of weeks, it is time to consider adding the fish. The choice is completely up to you but their are a few broad points to bear in mind before you go to your local aquarium dealer.

The quarantine tank

If possible, set up another tank equipped simply with a heater/thermostat, a box or sponge filter, thermometer and an airstone and use this as a quarantine aquarium. Place any new purchases into this tank first. Here, you can monitor new fishes for a week to ten days before adding them to your already established tank, thus reducing the chances of introducing any diseases.

Below: Introduce new fishes carefully to avoid stressing them. Float the unopened bag in the tank for up to 15 minutes before introducing some tank water into it and after a further five minutes you can gently release the fish.

Setting up a community aquarium

You may wish to set up a community aquarium. Other than the fact that the tank holds more than one fish, a community can be anything: a community of all one type of fish, a community of fish that all have the same color, or a community of totally different fishes. A theme often runs through a community. Fish from the same part of the world or fishes that would naturally live together are communities, as are tanks full of fishes with no relationship or connection to each other in any way.

It is a good idea to pick a mixture of fishes that will share different areas of the tank. Some species are surface-dwellers, others are mid-water swimmers, while others stay near the bottom. A mix of fishes from each of these groups gives a nice balance to a tank. Fish that normally shoal in the wild are best kept in small shoals and are happier like that, whereas fishes that are antisocial are best kept on their own. Obviously, fishes that have a taste for vegetable matter are best kept in tanks with plastic plants or no plants at all, whereas carnivorous fishes are best kept away from other fishes altogether or at least not with smaller, more vulnerable species.

Buying your fish

When you buy your first fishes they will probably be from your local dealer. Always check beforehand that the fishes in the shop are healthy. So what does a healthy fish look like? A healthy fish has good fins held erect and with no splits or white edges to them. The skin should be free of any pimples or white spots and there should be no sores or damaged areas. Avoid fish that hold their fins clamped to the body and closed up. Unless they are bottom-dwellers, fish should be swimming actively in midwater, but not with their heads up or down. Healthy fish do not swim with their mouths near the surface the whole time and they most definitely should not be gasping for air. There should be no other dead or sick-looking fish with the ones you intend to buy and there should also be no pieces of food or waste lying around in the tank.

Somebody in the shop will catch the fish for you and place them

Above: Setting up a mixed community of fishes provides color and variety in the aquarium. This tank has danios, livebearers - such as platies and guppies - and a gourami occupying the 'center stage' of this photograph. It is vital to mix compatible species and to create a balanced effect by choosing fishes that will occupy all levels within the tank. Many of the catfishes, for example, can create interest at the lower levels.

in a plastic bag with a little water in it. There only needs to be enough water to cover the fish completely and there should be a good pocket of air trapped in the top of the bag to keep the water oxygenated. The dealer should wrap this bag in paper to help keep it warm and dark on the journey home. If the fish you have bought are particularly small, then ask him to tie up the corners of the bag with rubber bands so that the fish cannot get trapped in them. You should take your fish home as soon as possible. If you have an insulated bag or a styrofoam box, place them in this for the journey to keep them warm. If you have other shops to visit while you are out, make your call to the aquarium shop the last stop before you start back home.

Acclimatizing your fishes

Once home, you need to acclimatize the fish. The water in your tank is likely to be at a slightly different temperature to that in the bag, so to equalize them, float the bag in the aquarium, unopened, for 10-15 minutes. After this period, open the bag carefully, and with a small cup pour some water from the tank into the bag. Wait another five minutes and then gently release the fish into the tank. If you feed the original fish in the tank at the same time, this will attract their attention and avoid them bothering your newcomers. All this helps to prevent sudden changes and reduce stress on the new fish.

How many fish can my tank hold?

The answer to this question is 'as many as you can squash into it', but they will not live! The real question should be 'How many fish will live healthily in my tank?'. This will not depend so much on the size of the tank but on the surface area. Fish breathe oxygen and this is absorbed into the aquarium mainly through the water surface. The greater the water surface area, the more oxygen the tank can absorb.

To work out how many fish your tank can hold, multiply the length of the two top edges together and this will give you the surface area. You should aim to have no more than 1in of fish length for every 10in^2 of surface area. For example, a tank that measures 36in x 15in has a water surface area of 540in^2. Dividing 540 by 10 produces a total recommended fish length of 54in. Therefore you could keep nine fishes each 6in long or 18 fishes each 3in long, for example.

This is only a very rough guide. Tanks with lots of plants and very strong water movement would hold more fish than a tank with no plants and little aeration. Try to keep as near to this guideline as possible and you will avoid problems with overcrowding. Always understock your tank rather than use up its full capacity.

New tank syndrome

The following sequence is common among beginners. Once set up, the tank is left running for a week or so. Then the aquarium is stocked with fish, possibly to its maximum capacity. Soon afterwards, fish start dying and the owner is at a loss to explain the cause. Eventually all, or nearly all, the fish die. In desperation, the aquarist strips the tank down, cleans the gravel and starts again, believing that it was some sort of disease that wiped out the fish. The same process is repeated and the fish die again.

There is no disease involved here. The basic problem is that the filtration system is not being given long enough to establish itself and break down waste. The fish then die from a build-up of nitrite. Washing all the gravel out at this stage simply destroys any useful aerobic bacteria that have developed. And the situation is usually exacerbated by the beginner's tendency to overfeed. The best course of action would be to do a partial water change and leave the tank for a further two weeks before beginning to introduce new fish gradually.

To avoid new tank syndrome from the outset, allow the tank to mature for at least two weeks, stock it with fish gradually, do not overstock and do not overfeed. Above all, be patient when setting up your first tank.

Feeding freshwater fish

Aquarium fishes will eat all types of foods, the only conditions are that the fish actually enjoys the food and that the pieces are small enough to be eaten. As with all animals, fish need to receive nutrients and vitamins essential for healthy growth. Fish also need to have a varied diet in order not to become bored with the same old foods and to avoid becoming addicted to one food, which is undesirable. It is important to offer foods of appropriate size. It is no good feeding tiny flakes of food to a great big fish, just as feeding large lumps of food to a tiny fish is useless.

The feeding routine

Generally you should feed your fish two or three times a day with very small helpings - unless they are large carnivores, in which case they will have special requirements and these are dealt with individually later on in the book. If you are feeding flake food, then give them only a very small pinch and check that this is all eaten within three to five minutes. Healthy fish are hungry fish. If your fish are always at the surface looking for food, or if they rush to the surface when you approach the tank, then that is a good sign. If you are giving your fish the messier foods, such as blended meats or raw fish, then this should all be consumed within a minute or it will pollute the tank. A quite common practice is to 'fast' the fish for one day a week. This ensures a better appetite and the fish will not be harmed; in their natural state they can go weeks without food .

Flakes and pellets

Flake foods are a convenient way of feeding aquarium fishes. There are flakes of different colors that contain various ingredients such as fish, roe, wheat, meat, vegetables, trace elements and vitamins. Feed only a small amount to your fish at any one time. Flake foods are fine for fish up to 4-5in in length, but you will need something else to supplement them when they grow larger. Pellets have roughly the same ingredients as flake foods but are more substantial. They are available in various sizes and shapes, whether floating or sinking; some promote color, others promote growth.

Live foods

There are many live foods available to aquarists and your dealer should stock at least one or two that you will find suitable. Among these are water fleas (*Daphnia*), small crustaceans that should be available all year round. You can also buy brineshrimps (*Artemia*) - small shrimps that live naturally in saline lakes; simply rinse these

Above: Aquarium dealers supply water fleas and bloodworms (Chironomus - in the pinkish water) in plastic bags. Simply strain the water away through a piece of muslin or cloth before feeding them to your fish. If you keep the bags in a cool place they should last about a week. Brineshrimps and river shrimps are also supplied in this form.

Tubifex worms

Tubifex are tiny worms that thrive in polluted streams and rivers. Do not feed them to your fish even if you clean the worms a thousand times over, because they are full of disease-causing bacteria. If you would like to feed *Tubifex* to your fish, buy the freeze-dried or frozen forms, which are totally safe.

Live foods for free

There are plenty of free live foods in the garden. Your fish will eat virtually anything that moves, provided it is of a suitable size. Wood lice are taken greedily by large fish and there can be no better food for tropical fish than earthworms.

Common frozen foods

Bloodworm

Tubifex

Daphnia

Brineshrimp

Beef

Above: This is a representative selection of frozen foods prepared for aquarium fish. The benefits of using such foods is that they are completely free of disease-causing organisms or parasites and are supplied in flat frozen sheets that are easy to break up and use.

Flakes and pellets

Small floating pellets

Large color-enhancer pellets

Balanced flake food

Floating foodsticks for large fish

and feed them to your fishes. Also look out for river shrimps; these are too big for small fish, but large carnivorous fish relish them. Aquarium fish also enjoy bloodworms - red aquatic larvae from river mud. These are excellent for bringing fish into breeding condition.

Freeze-dried and frozen foods
Freeze-dried versions of the above live foods make safe and nutritious supplements to flake foods. Other freeze-dried foods include *Mysis* shrimp, Pacific shrimp, *Tubifex* worms, krill and plankton. These foods are also available in frozen form. Store these foods in the freezer and thaw out as much as you need each day.

Meaty foods
Beef heart is good for carnivorous fish. To prepare this, trim off the fat, blend the meat to a puree and then freeze it in thin slabs that you can easily break up into pieces as you need them. You can also do this with chicken, turkey, fish or any other non-fatty meats.

Vegetable foods
Many fish enjoy some vegetable matter in their diet, including blanched lettuce, garden peas with the skins popped off, and even baked beans. There is no harm in trying various vegetables - but be sure to remove them from the tank swiftly if the fish ignore them.

Home-made general-purpose diet

Blend the following ingredients together to form a balanced diet that you can feed three times a day, every day if you wish. You can vary the ingredients slightly to suit your fishes' taste.

4 oz ox heart
4 oz white fish
2 oz processed peas
2 oz baked beans
2 oz spinach
2 tablespoonfuls of flake food.

Chop the ox heart and the fish into small chunks and carefully blend to a puree in a liquidizer or blender. Now comes the messy bit! Scrape the outer skins off the peas and beans and add the insides to the ox heart and fish mixture. Add the spinach and flake and mix all the ingredients in a bowl. Spoon the mixture into small plastic bags and roll each bag out until it is about an eighth of an inch thick. Place the bags in the freezer overnight. Next day, all the bags will have frozen and will be ready for use. Simply snap off a small piece of the frozen slab and drop it into the aquarium where you normally feed the fish. The food will quickly thaw in the tank, although many fish will try, and may succeed, to eat it frozen.

Freeze-dried foods

Tablets - ideal as treats

White shrimp

Tubifex cubes

Krill - a good supplement

Maintaining your aquarium

Above: This air-driven 'vacuum cleaner' is a useful cleaning device. The rising stream of air bubbles causes water to flow up the tube and through the net bag, where debris is strained off.

Aquarium fishes need to be looked after, but the amount of care they need is very small indeed. The best idea is to set aside a certain time each week for 'doing the tank'.

Maintaining water quality

One of the most important regular tasks is to check and maintain the water quality in the aquarium. Fish waste products produce ammonia, which eventually breaks down to become nitrite - a very poisonous substance indeed that is dangerous to fish in any quantity. If your filtration system is working properly, hardly any nitrite will form in the aquarium, but in order to make sure it doesn't, and to remove other harmful chemicals that are not eliminated by the action of bacteria in the so-called 'nitrogen cycle', it is vital to make regular water changes. A water change should be between 10 and 15 percent of the tank volume. To judge how much water this involves measure the height of your tank, divide it by ten and make a small mark this far from the top with a marker pen. Then you will know just how much water to remove each time.

The easiest way to remove the water is to siphon it out. To do this, fill a length of tubing with water - the wider the diameter, the faster the flow - cover both ends with your thumbs and carry it to the tank. Place one end below the water surface and remove your thumb. Place the other end in a bucket or out of the front door and remove your other thumb. A siphonic flow will now begin and continue until you remove the tube from the tank. If you hold the end of the tube just above the gravel then the water flow will also carry away debris. You can buy a gravel washer that digs into the gravel and draws any waste out by siphonic action.

Now replenish the tank with new water, which should be as near to the temperature of the aquarium water as you can possibly manage. The best way to do this is to pre-store some water in a clean bucket in a warm place for a couple of days. This will not only get it up to the right temperature but will also allow the chlorine in the tap

Testing for nitrite levels

Nitrite test kits work on a dye method and of all the test kits to buy, this is the most useful and cost effective. Nitrite is tested in parts per million (ppm), which is equivalent to milligrams per liter (mg/l). Either way, your kit will clearly indicate if your water has a dangerous level of nitrite. If it has, you must make an immediate water change. Check that your biological filtration system is working well and if this is fine then you are either overfeeding or your tank is overstocked. Another possibility is that there is a dead fish somewhere in the tank.

Do not confuse nitrite with nitrate. Nitrate is the step after ammonia and nitrite in the 'nitrogen cycle' (see the diagram of this cycle shown on page 14) and, although harmful in quantity, it is not as poisonous as nitrite.

Acidity and alkalinity

Tests kits are available for measuring the acid/alkaline balance of the water and most work on a color dye principle. The scale used is pH, which runs from pH0 (very acid) to pH14 (very alkaline), with pH7 as neutral. Either side of the neutral point the scale is logarithmic, so that pH6 is ten times more acidic than pH7 and pH5 a hundred times more acidic than pH7.

The pH values of natural fresh water sources vary from about pH6 for the soft acidic water of an Amazonian river to about pH8.5 for the hard alkaline water of Lake Tanganyika in Africa. Some of the less tolerant fishes from these environments only flourish if the pH value of their tank water reflects the conditions in their habitat.

The safest way to make your water more acid or alkaline is to use a pH adjuster from your aquarium shop. There are other ways, such as filtering through peat to increase acidity, but these methods are a bit 'hit or miss' and may stress your fish.

water to dissipate. Chlorine is added to tap water by the water company as a disinfectant and is harmful to fishes. Therefore, any water going into the aquarium should be allowed to stand for at least 24 hours or treated with a proprietary dechlorinator. Add the water gently, trying not to disturb the bottom of the tank and thereby upsetting the fish. Properly carried out, fish actually enjoy water changes, they sparkle more, their growth rate is enhanced, they become more active and it really 'replenishes their batteries'.

Certain fish are fussy about whether the water is hard or soft, and some are more sensitive to the acid/alkaline balance of the water. Fortunately, most popular aquarium fishes are undemanding and adapt to whatever conditions they encounter. As a beginner, it is far better and safer to leave well alone, but as you advance you may want to tinker with the water quality to get it nearer to the ideal.

Cleaning up and regular checks

Other jobs to do at this point are to trim and replant any plants that have not stayed rooted. Use a sharp pair of scissors for trimming leaves and the blunt end of any long implement, such as a knitting needle, to push plants back into the gravel. Also remove any algae that has grown on the glass using an algae scraper. If you buy one of the magnetic types, make sure you do not trap any particles of gravel between the plates or they will scratch the glass.

You should also check your electrical wiring and see that there are no faults. Check the water temperature every day and watch your fish carefully for five minutes for signs of disease or odd behavior.

Above: Scouring pads on long handles such as this one make cleaning the inside glass of the aquarium relatively easy, at least in fairly small tanks.

Below: Magnetic glass cleaners are useful for deeper tanks, where access to the lower areas is difficult. Moving the outer magnetic block drags the inside one across the glass and the plastic brushlike surface scrapes off any algae.

Essential accessories for maintaining your tank

Algae scraper
Use these to scrape any algae from the glass. Some are like little scouring pads which can be fitted onto long handles. Another type is like a plastic trowel on a stick and works very well. You can fit a razor blade to this type but be sure not to go near the silicone sealant with it, damaging this can cause a very nasty leak! The most ingenious type consists of two magnets that cling together through the glass so that as you pull the outer one the inner one cleans away the algae.

Tubing
You will need some wide-bore plastic tubing, say 0.5in, to siphon water out of the tank.

Gravel cleaner
This device fits onto the end of your siphon tubing and digs into the gravel while you siphon water out. As the dirt comes out of the gravel, the gravel drops back so that only dirt and not gravel is removed in the flow of water. Some gravel cleaners have a pump action to start the siphon flow (see page 93).

Net for removing fish
It would be wise to buy at least one, if not two nets from the outset. Try to pick a soft net and one that is a little larger than half the tank's width.

What makes water hard or soft?

Tap water contains salts of minerals, especially calcium and magnesium, that make the water 'hard'. There are two types of water hardness: general, or permanent; and carbonate, or temporary, hardness. A popular scale used for hardness is °dH, with 3°dH being considered soft and over 25°dH as hard. To measure hardness use the relevant test kit, which usually involves adding drops of a colored liquid to a sample of tank water until there is a color change.

The only way to remove general hardness from water is to pass it through a suitable water softener. Carbonate hardness can be lowered partially by boiling and also by passing it through a filter with peat in it. Other ways of softening water include adding distilled water or rain water.

To harden water, add small amounts of sodium bicarbonate or magnesium sulfate. But do it in small amounts so that the changes occur very gradually! Remember, sudden changes can kill fish.

Anatomy and health care

It is worth getting to know the basic anatomy of a fish in case you need to describe an injury or disease symptom to a veterinarian or dealer; if you know the names of the external parts of the body it will help you to pinpoint the problem more accurately. Another reason is that books often describe the shapes of fishes and if you know which particular fins or parts of the body they are referring to, you will have a basic idea of what the fish looks like even without seeing an illustration or photograph.

Fish parasites

Fish parasites are generally regarded as larger life forms living on the body of a fish. Parasites are rare in aquarium fishes and usually only occur on wild-caught species that have been imported.

Gill flukes

Gill flukes are like tiny worms that anchor themselves to the fish's gills, causing respiratory problems and, eventually, death. Suspect gill flukes if a fish begins to swim at the water surface gasping for air. Treat with a mild parasiticide, but first make sure that the water is being oxygenated properly and that the biological filter is working correctly.

Skin flukes

Instead of anchoring themselves to the gills, these flukes attach to the skin. They can be removed with tweezers or a parasiticide.

Fish lice

Fish lice such as *Argulus* resemble miniature tortoises on the fish's body. Remove them carefully with tweezers.

Basic fish anatomy

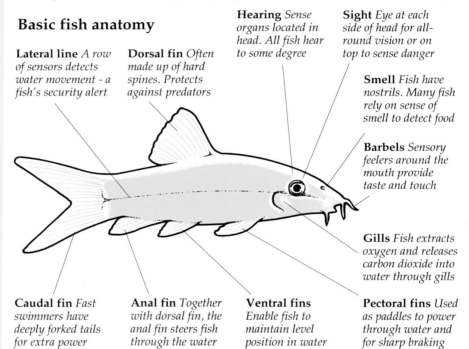

Lateral line *A row of sensors detects water movement - a fish's security alert*

Dorsal fin *Often made up of hard spines. Protects against predators*

Hearing *Sense organs located in head. All fish hear to some degree*

Sight *Eye at each side of head for all-round vision or on top to sense danger*

Smell *Fish have nostrils. Many fish rely on sense of smell to detect food*

Barbels *Sensory feelers around the mouth provide taste and touch*

Gills *Fish extracts oxygen and releases carbon dioxide into water through gills*

Caudal fin *Fast swimmers have deeply forked tails for extra power*

Anal fin *Together with dorsal fin, the anal fin steers fish through the water*

Ventral fins *Enable fish to maintain level position in water*

Pectoral fins *Used as paddles to power through water and for sharp braking*

Diseases and stress

The majority of fish diseases are caused through stress. So how are fish put under stress? Sad to say, most fish are put under stress by their owners or visitors to the house. People tapping on the front glass, temperatures being allowed to rise and fall, or a poor mixture of fish in which one or two are bullies and the others are bullied all contribute to stress. If fish are not put under these types of stress, then the chances of them contracting disease are dramatically reduced. Look for signs of stress in the tank on a regular basis. Are the fish nervous? Is one fish chasing all the others about? Does the temperature fluctuate or does it stay too low? If you can remedy these situations diseases will occur much less frequently.

Above: Although more commonly encountered on coldwater fishes, this fish louse (Argulus) has attached itself to a swordtail - a tropical species. The louse grows up to 0.4in across and clings on firmly with twin suckers.

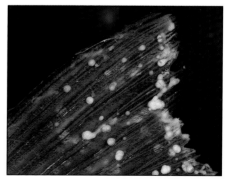

Above: White spot (Ichthyophthirius) appears as tiny white spots, each one a cyst that eventually bursts to send its single-celled, or protozoal, parasites into the tank, where they will affect the other fishes with potentially fatal results.

Common diseases

White spot (*Ichthyophthirius*)
White spots that increase in number. Responds to treatment. Eliminate stress-causing factors.

Velvet (*Oodinium*)
Rusty coloring to skin and clamping up of fins. Effective proprietary remedies available.

Bloat
Fish swells up and does not eat. Investigate water conditions and diet. Treat with antibacterial and remove sick fish from tank.

Popeye
A condition in which one or both eyes protrude from head. Can be due to injury or bacterial infection. Seek veterinary help.

Hole-in-the-head
Small holes appear on head and body. Often affects cichlids. Cures are slow and expensive. Improve tank conditions.

Fungus
Growths like absorbent cotton. Treat with fungicide. Check water conditions/temperature.

Mouth fungus
Attacks lips and mouth. Often seen in cyprinids. Responds to fungicide. Check stress factors.

Finrot
Bacteria attack damaged fins. Use an antibacterial or add salt if the fish will tolerate this.

Symptoms of disease

Fish will always show symptoms of disease at an early stage. Signs to look for include fish holding their fins tightly clamped to the body (often referred to as being 'closed up'), fish swimming with the head near to the surface all the time, fish swimming with the head up or down, loss of color, ragged fins, scales sticking out or dropping off, and a general loss of appetite and condition.

What do I do immediately if these symptoms appear?

Several fish gasping at the surface and breathing fast

❑ Check to see that the airstone is functioning and that there is good water movement in the tank.

❑ Check that the undergravel filter is functioning properly.

❑ See that heater has not stuck on.

❑ Perform a 30% water change.

❑ If after a water change these symptoms persist, the fish may be suffering from gill flukes. Isolate the fish if possible and treat them with a suitable remedy.

Fish holding its fins clamped to the body (i.e 'closed up')

❑ Check the heater function and that the temperature is correct.

❑ See that nothing has been added to the aquarium that might be poisonous, including aerosols possibly sprayed near the tank.

❑ If you have checked and cleared the above, make a 30% water change and use a mild bactericide.

Fish dying and swimming in a 'whirling' pattern

❑ These are classic signs of poisoning. Perform a 50% water change and locate the source of the problem. This may be a poisonous rock or object in the tank, which you must remove.

Fish rubbing themselves against rocks and 'flicking'

❑ Several possible causes, such as white spot, external parasites or an irritant in the water.

❑ Inspect the fish closely. If white spots or parasites are present on the skin, treat them appropriately with a suitable remedy.

❑ If all looks well on the fishes' skin perform a 30% water change. If the symptoms decrease after this, suspect the presence of some irritant in the aquarium.

❑ If symptoms increase after the water change, suspect something wrong with your tap water or conditioner. Is there too much chlorine in the water or are you overdosing with dechlorinator?

The hospital tank

If you have a spare tank or one used for quarantining new fish then it will be useful for isolating sick or injured fish. Set this tank up with just a heater/thermostat and thermometer, plus an airstone. It will not need a filter, as sick and injured fish will not be fed for the short time they are in the tank. Transfer any fish found to be sick, injured or carrying a parasitic infestation to this tank and treat them in isolation from the community tank. Some form of opaque cover is a good idea, so that you can reduce the light - often helpful during treatment.

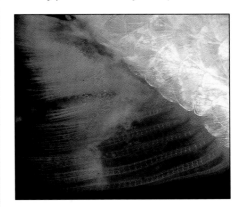

Below: The milky-white growths of fungus show clearly on the anal fin of this fish. Fungal spores can invade damaged tissue and broken scales; healthy fish are usually well protected.

Breeding your fishes

Breeding fish yourself is highly satisfying, and it is rewarding to raise fish for virtually nothing except a little time and effort. Many freshwater tropical fishes will breed in the aquarium, and those most frequently spawned in tanks include livebearers, cichlids, catfishes, barbs among cyprinids, tetras among characins, and anabantids.

All these fish have different modes of reproduction. Livebearers release live fry, cichlids deposit eggs on a substrate and either guard them or take them up into their mouths, whereas catfishes may deposit eggs and abandon them or guard them. Tetras and barbs usually scatter their eggs, and anabantids make bubblenests and deposit the eggs within these floating rafts of bubbles to hatch. Nevertheless, there are many practical points common to all these fish when it comes to inducing them to spawn.

Getting the fishes to spawn

Simulating the fish's natural environment is the first and most important factor in getting them to breed. If a fish comes from a soft acidic river, it will (in most cases) require soft acidic water in the aquarium if it is to breed. There are exceptions to this rule, and with the constant breeding of fish in the aquarium they are gradually evolving to accept breeding conditions that are further from their natural ones. Generally speaking, however, if you get the water right you are halfway to breeding success.

Next, consider the surroundings. If a fish is used to living in densely planted waters where the sunlight is filtered through overhanging branches, then a heavily planted aquarium with subdued lighting is likely to be just right. These fish may be very timid in other conditions and unless they can settle and feel comfortable they are not going to breed. Too much activity near the

Above: Among the cichlids, angelfishes are particularly easy to breed in the aquarium. First signs of a pair developing are two fish snatching brief moments with each other away from the pack, pecking at a rock or leaf together and making strange little flicks of the head. It is best to place this pair in a tank of their own. After anything from a day to a few weeks, the female starts to develop a small tube just in front of her anal fin. This egg tube, or ovipositor, is clearly visible in the above photograph. The male develops a tube, but this is more pointed and not as broad. The pair select and peck clean a small patch on a vertical rock or leaf and eventually the female will start laying eggs on it.

Above: The male follows and fertilizes the eggs. The female fans them with her pectoral fins and pecks off any infertile eggs that have turned white with fungus, and they hatch after two or three days. The fry are then stuck by little filaments to another leaf or rock until they are free-swimming. At this stage, feed them with plenty of newly hatched brineshrimp four or five times a day until they are large enough to eat crumbled flake food. The parents should continue to guard the fry for several more weeks, but due to constant inbreeding they are often bad parents and eat their own young or eggs. You can hatch the eggs away from the parents in a separate tank using light aeration from an airstone to replace the fishes fanning and a mild bactericide to replace the fishes' cleaning habits.

Below: A proud male paradisefish (Macropodus opercularis) *keeps an eye on the bubblenest he has created at the water surface by blowing air bubbles into a sticky mass. Often, fragments of plants are incorporated into the nest to make it quite a bulky affair. This species among anabantid fishes is ideal for beginners to breed because it will adapt to a wide range of aquarium conditions. It is fascinating to watch the spawning ritual as the male entwines around the female below the nest. Eggs released by the female are fertilized by the male and gathered up into the nest. The tiny fry hatch in about 24-36 hours and will flourish on liquid food or infusorians.*

tank will also be a deterrent to spawning, so keep things peaceful.

In the wild, fishes are usually induced into spawning by some natural stimuli, such as heavy rain. This swells and cools the rivers, increases the oxygen content and washes an abundance of insect and animal life into the water. You can imitate the effect of heavy rain by making slightly larger, more frequent water changes using cooler water. You can make this even more authentic by lowering the water level gradually over a period of a few days. To mimic the high degree of organic matter washed into the water during heavy rain you can add an aquarium tonic, and increased feedings of live foods such as brineshrimps will act as the abundance of insect life that becomes available at this time. After this cooling period of rain, the waters warm up and you can simulate this by turning up the adjustment on the heater/thermostat a degree or two. Increasing the aeration will give the impression that the water is moving faster, and when all these actions are taken together the fish are often 'tricked' into believing that their captive environment is entirely natural.

Raising the fry

Raising the fry can be easy with many species but almost impossible with others. Newly hatched brineshrimps will often be sufficient for

their needs, providing the fry are of a reasonable size (pinhead or larger), but smaller fry will need smaller foods. Proprietary liquid fry foods are good, but also consider raising infusoria as a first food. These are single-celled creatures that live on decaying vegetable matter. Start a culture by placing potato peelings in a jar and filling this with hot, nearly boiling water. Leave this in a warm sunlit place. After a couple of days the culture will go cloudy and in another few days it will clear again. Once cleared, you can harvest the tiny creatures by simply pouring small amounts of the liquid into the fry tank. Feed the fry little and often, 4-5 times a day. As they grow, wean them onto hard-boiled egg yolk and then finely crumbled flake foods.

Above: A midas, or lemon, cichlid (Cichlasoma citrinellum) *with a shoal of fry staying close for protection. This Central American cichlid will breed readily in the aquarium, although not without a degree of drama during the proceedings. The male may be so aggressive in his courtship that it might be best to separate the pair either side of a glass partition with a small gap at the bottom. As the female lays her eggs on one side of the partition, the male produces sperm on the other side, but enough can flow under the glass to fertilize at least some of the eggs. If the pair are not separated, they will lay about 600-800 eggs on a suitably flat rock. The female digs a pit nearby and the newly hatched fry are placed in this 'nursery' for the first few days. Both parents watch over and protect the fry.*

FRESHWATER FISHES FOR YOUR AQUARIUM

Walking into a specialist tropical fish shop and being faced with the bewildering array of fishes on offer can be a daunting prospect. Which fishes can I keep together? What do they eat? Which ones will eat each other? This section of the book deals with each of the main groups of freshwater fishes that you are likely to encounter. It includes not only examples of small fishes that will safely live together, but also discusses large cichlids and catfishes that are best housed on their own or in a single species tank.

A general overview of each group is followed by photographs of representative species described in more detail. There is not a single group of which one could say that any fish within it is suitable for a community tank - there is always at least one exception to the rule. If in doubt about the identity of a fish, ask the shopkeeper. Most are willing and able to give sound advice - after all, it is in their interest to help you so that you return to buy more stock. And if you don't ask, you may find that that very attractive 2in fish grows at an alarming rate and becomes a 12in drab-colored bully that uproots every plant in the aquarium and kills or eats several of the inmates!

Details of the breeding requirements of many of the fishes are included, and although these may not be of major concern at first, you may find that the fish breed without you having to lift a finger. If you happen to be lucky and your fishes multiply, this could well be the beginning of a long association with this fascinating hobby.

Characins

This group of fishes comes mainly from the Southern American continent, with a lesser number originating in Africa. They are quite varied in size and shape, and diverse in their behavior and feeding habits. Some members of the Characidae have a small fleshy adipose fin, but this feature is absent in groups such as the pencilfishes (see page 40). Some of these fishes are very gentle and not in the least aggressive towards each other - or other fishes for that matter - while at the other end of the spectrum is the piranha, a characin renowned for its ferocity. Most characins shoal in nature and also frequently breed in great shoals. More often than not, characins come from the slow-moving rivers of the rainforests, where the water has a tannic quality and is usually soft and acidic. Many are carnivorous, but most are omnivorous, taking a wide range of foods.

Tetras

Tetras are some of the smallest and most beautiful aquarium fishes; in fact, they include some of the smallest fishes in the world. Nearly all tetras are shoaling fish in nature and will shoal in the aquarium too, if given the chance. Shoaling is their form of protection. Should a predator attack the shoal then the sudden movement of one fish triggers a panic reaction throughout the shoal. With all the fish moving in different directions at the same time, the hope is that the predator will miss its prey and the tetras will escape. That is the theory, but it does not always work in practice. Many tetras are naturally insectivorous and appreciate being offered small live foods in the aquarium. They make ideal community fish and will live peacefully with all other fishes. They are midwater swimmers and feeders and very active - in fact, they are continuously on the go. In a gentle mixed community, *Corydoras* catfishes, livebearers and other small, non-aggressive fish make good tankmates for tetras.

A typical tetra tank should contain plenty of plants, thickly packed around the back and sides of the tank, with a large clearing in the middle. Tetras do not seem to mind whether the tank lighting is bright or subdued. They are not timid, provided they are kept in small shoals of five or more. Ideally, the water in their tank should be soft and acidic, which you can achieve by filtering the water through peat and using plenty of bogwood for decor. However, tetras will do very well in all water compositions, as long as the water is kept clean by making regular partial water changes of about 15 percent of the aquarium capacity. When carrying out water changes, make sure that the temperature does not drop very much, as tetras are less hardy than some other aquarium fishes.

Left: Neon tetras (Paracheirodon innesi) *originate from the Amazon and only grow to about 1.5in or a little more. They are among the slimmest tetras and are renowned for their colors. The top of the back is olive green and below this runs an electric blue line from the top of the tail through the eye. Below this line is a bright silver belly and behind this is a bright blood-red anal section. Neon tetras eat most flake foods, along with freeze-dried* Tubifex, *brineshrimp and* Daphnia, *although they much prefer frozen foods or, better still, live foods. The water should be soft and acidic if possible, but neon tetras will be quite happy in medium-hard water that is neutral or very slightly alkaline. The temperature in the aquarium should be kept at about 77°F.*

Left: *The Amazonian glowlight tetra* (Hemigrammus erythrozonus) *is another interesting addition to most peaceful communities. It grows to an absolute maximum of 2in and then only rarely. Its long, slim body is quite transparent, with a glowing orange line running along it. This color is also evident at the base of the dorsal fin and all the fins have touches of white on the edges. Like all tetras, it likes to shoal if possible and makes an attractive display if kept in a large group. Glowlight tetras prefer well-lit, heavily planted tanks with plenty of other small, peaceful fish for company. They happily accept most foods, but prefer live foods.*

Below: *The beautiful Congo tetras* (Phenacogrammus interruptus) *grow to about 3.5in and adults have very long flowing fins. The specimens shown here have yet to develop their adult finnage. All the fins, especially the tail, the anal fin and the pectoral fins, have a ragged appearance and a whitish edge. These fins are even longer in males than in females and look really stunning. The mouth is quite large for the fish's size. Congo tetras are peaceful, although they may chase fish smaller than themselves. They require a tank measuring at least 36in, but 48in would be better, and will live quite happily in soft water at a temperature of 72-75°F.*

Breeding tetras in the home aquarium

Tetras are not always willing to spawn in the aquarium. Those that do, require soft, acidic water and a temperature of about 78°F. At one end of a breeding tank place a bunch of fine-leaved plants held together with plant wire, and weigh this down with a stone. No gravel is required in the tank. Select a well-fed pair of tetras in top condition, put them in the tank in the evening and leave them alone with no artificial lighting, just room light. If all goes well, the pair will spawn the following morning. Swimming into the plants together, the female lays her eggs as the male fertilizes them. The eggs will stick to the plant leaves as they settle upon them. Remove the parents after all the eggs have been laid, otherwise they will methodically go over the plants and eat their own eggs. In most cases, the eggs hatch in a little over a day and the fry are free-swimming a few days later, but they may be very difficult to see as they are so small. Probably the first signs of the fry will be tiny, glassy, silver hairs stuck to the tank glass. The really difficult part starts now, and that is keeping the tiny fry alive. The best food is an especially prepared fry food for egglayers. Most aquarium shops can supply this in a tube, rather like liquid toothpaste. As the fry progress, they can be weaned onto newly hatched brineshrimps until they are large enough to feed on very finely crushed flake food.

Above: The West African red-eyed charcin, or Arnold's characin, (Arnoldichthys spilopterus) is completely peaceful and makes an ideal community fish. The Congo tetra is a particularly good tankmate; do not keep it with aggressive or spiteful fishes. Some of the scales on this fish are dark, creating a lattice pattern. The quite tall, square dorsal fin has a black to charcoal gray blotch in the middle, and a black line runs horizontally through the tail. The body colors are quite subtle, the top half being purple and brown, the bottom yellow and green. Males tend to be far more splendid in coloration than the females. This fish has all the same requirements as other African tetras.

Left: *The distinctive phantom tetras - this one is the black phantom tetra - (Megalamphodus megalopterus) are excellent fish for a peaceful community aquarium containing fish that are not too large. They grow to about 1.6in and like to shoal, so keep them in small groups. Provide the same water conditions as for other tetras and a similar diet, including live foods and freeze-dried brineshrimps. Dense plants or thickets of fine-leaved plants, such as* Cabomba *make the fish feel at home.*

Below: *The bleeding heart tetra, or tetra Perez, (Hyphessobrycon erythrostigma) is a really beautiful Amazonian tetra and is easy to keep, provided its tankmates are neither aggressive nor so small that they may fit in the bleeding heart's mouth. It is happiest if kept in a shoal in soft, acidic water, but usually does very well in ordinary tap water that has not been adjusted in any way. It relishes live foods, but accepts flake and freeze-dried foods as well. Provide a varied diet.*

Hatchetfishes

Several types of hatchetfish form another little group of very popular fishes. The main apparent difference between them is their coloration, otherwise they require much the same in terms of care and feeding. Hatchetfishes are surface-feeders and dwellers. They can rise progressively above the surface in much the same way as a hydrofoil and often skim over the surface of the water for up to 6.5ft. This is because they have developed long pectoral fins that they can 'beat' like wings. Be sure to attach a very tightly fitting cover over any tank containing hatchetfishes. The most commonly seen species in the aquarium hobby is the silver hatchetfish (*Gasteropelecus sternicla*). It grows to about 2.6in and thrives in soft, slightly acidic water at about 79°F. Live food will keep the fish healthy and active.

Pencilfishes

Pencilfishes are very slim with pointed mouths. All require similar care and water conditions. They originate from the soft waters of the South American rainforests, so set up their tank accordingly. There are many species of pencilfishes available in the aquarium hobby; your choice will depend on what your dealer can supply.

Piranhas and pacus

It may seem hard to believe that piranhas should be related to the gentle little fishes that make up the majority of the characin group, but it is true. At up to 12in long, piranhas are very much larger than tetras, but do not deserve the nasty reputation they have acquired over the years. In the aquarium, at least, the piranha is a relatively shy, retiring creature. Stories of piranhas in the dark Amazonian rainforests reducing cattle to skeletons in minutes are true, but this occurs in a river system where piranhas live in great shoals of 300 fishes or more and become very hungry. Many people keep piranhas with a sort of morbid fascination for what might happen, and give the impression that they would be quite pleased if the fish bit them as evidence of their macho capabilities! Keep young piranhas in a tank at least 48in long, but provide a larger aquarium as they grow. Similar in shape to piranhas and also from northern South America, the pacus can also be kept in a large tank with plenty of shelter.

Below: The three-lined pencilfish (Nannostomus trifasciatus) is a small, very peaceful fish from South America that grows to about 2in. Small tetras, livebearers and Corydoras catfishes are ideal partners for it in the aquarium. The pencilfish's body shape is very long and slim, with a pointed snout and tiny mouth. Ideally, the water should be kept at about 79°F and be soft and very slightly acidic. The fish enjoys live foods, but it will eat frozen, as well as freeze-dried and flake food.

Right: The black pacu (Piaractus brachypomum) from northern South America, is a real giant that grows to over 18in long. It is a fruit-eater, enjoying any fruit or vegetable, but it is not a vegetarian; pacus will eat virtually anything that is put into the tank. They are large, laterally compressed fish, with a black back, gray belly and red-orange throat. Aquarium water should be soft and acidic and kept very clean. Pacus are shoaling fish in their natural habitat, but a group in captivity will need a very large tank. A single fish in a 'pet tank' often becomes friendly towards its owners.

Cyprinids

Cyprinids are very widespread throughout the world. The group includes some of the more familiar aquarium species, such as barbs, and also many of the common non-tropicals, such as goldfish and carp. These species vary greatly in size; some barbs only grow to 3in or less, whereas some of the larger carp can grow to over 24in and weigh as much as 50lb. Many of these fish prefer to live in shoals, although they can become 'loners' to quite an extent as they get older. Very often, they have an appetite for vegetable matter, so plants within their aquarium may be subject to attack. You may not notice what is happening until the plants begin to look ragged or disappear entirely. Even then, you may suspect another source of attack, such as snails, before identifying the seemingly harmless barb as the culprit. Another frequent and annoying habit of some cyprinids is nipping the fins of other fishes, particularly those with long flowing finnage or extended fins, such as angelfish, for instance. Bear this in mind when choosing tankmates.

Cyprinids are egg-scatterers. When they spawn, they go through an elaborate ritual in which the male chases and nudges the female throughout the tank, until he eventually persuades her into a densely planted area, where the eggs are released and fertilized, finally dropping among the fine leaves and sticking to them. No parental protection is afforded to the young; indeed, if the parents stumble on eggs or young they are likely to eat them.

Most cyprinids are undemanding and easy to care for. They usually prefer soft, slightly acidic water, but will do very well in most types of water, as long as it is kept clean. Carry out frequent partial water changes and maintain a temperature in the region of 75°F. These fish are not worried by bright lighting conditions, and if kept in shoals will frequent the open waters, rarely distracted by the goings-on outside the aquarium, unless it is feeding time!

Barbs

While many barbs are deep-bodied, solid and carplike in appearance, other species are long and slim. They vary in size from 2-16in and most are happiest living in a shoal and should be kept in small groups in the aquarium. They have small, slightly underslung mouths. Most enjoy vegetable matter and will nibble at aquarium plants, so provide alternative green food, such as lettuce and peas.

Below: The tiger, or Sumatran, barb (Barbus tetrazona) *only reaches about 2in in the home aquarium. These delightful, colorful little fish like to shoal, so keep them in small groups. They appreciate clean, clear water with a temperature of about 77°F. Tiger barbs eat live foods, such as brineshrimp or* Daphnia *and seize frozen, freeze-dried and flake foods in little raids to the surface. Add some vegetable matter to their diet.*

Below: The clown barb (Barbus everetti) is so-called because its markings are like that of a clown's costume. It is one of the slightly larger barbs, growing to a little over 5in, although males are slightly smaller. A shoal will need a tank measuring at least 36in long to give them plenty of space to swim around. Like many barbs, clown barbs nibble at soft-leaved plants in the aquarium, so either stock the tank with plastic plants, or rely on rocks and bogwood for decoration or add a variety of vegetable matter to their diet. Clown barbs like a water temperature of about 77°F and soft water if possible. They are one of the more difficult species to induce to spawn in captivity.

Above: The shoaling rosy barbs (Barbus conchonius) are excellent community fishes. In nature they are found in rivers, ponds and backwaters in northern India, Bengal and Assam. Their coloration is best seen in reflected light in a 36in tank. Males are gold to olive-green along the back with pink flanks, their fins are tinged with pink and the dorsal fin has a deep black tip. Females are gold to olive-green all over, with a very slight flush of pink on the flanks. When in breeding condition, the males take on a deep red color as they chase the egg-scattering females through thickets of plants. It is difficult to determine the sexes of young fish, as their colors only begin to develop as they mature. They are sexually mature at about 2.4in and do not usually exceed 4in in the aquarium. The tank should have plenty of fine-leaved plants and ample swimming space. Provide soft, slightly acidic water, with a pH level of 6.5. The fish will thrive at a temperature of 64-72°F. They accept flake, freeze-dried, frozen and live foods.

Danios and rasboras

Danios and rasboras are some of the most popular of the small, gentle community fishes and perhaps the least aggressive of all aquarium fishes. They are easy to maintain, although not very robust. Most remain towards the upper layer of the water and so complement fishes that frequent the lower waters, such as catfishes and loaches. Providing they are fed small, frequent meals and are not housed with larger aggressive fish, they remain trouble-free and are excellent beginners' fish.

Above: The zebra, or striped danio, (Brachydanio rerio) *from eastern India and Bangladesh only grows to a total length of 2in, although females are a little larger. They have a long, slim body with a blue to olive base color and an overlay of four bright yellow, horizontal stripes. Both the anal and caudal fin also have these stripes. Their attractive appearance makes them a very popular choice for the gentle community aquarium. These fish accept a variety of foods, including all the usual freeze-dried and frozen foods, but as they only have tiny mouths they can only take tiny pieces. Freeze-dried or live mosquito larvae are often available from your dealer in summer and these make a very natural diet for these fishes. Zebras are hardy and make no special demands, so make suitable subjects for the newcomer to the fishkeeping hobby.*

Left: The pearl danio (Brachydanio albolineatus) from the dark, muddy rivers of Burma and Indo-China is a superb beginner's fish. These lovely little fishes are quite hardy for their size - only 2in - and very active, which makes them interesting aquarium subjects. The body is very long and slim, all the fins are clear and the fish feeds from the surface with its small, upturned mouth. Towards the back half of the body are two or three pink lines that run horizontally over pastel blue scales to produce a pearl effect, hence the common name. This species also has a golden form. Males are usually more brightly colored and not as plump as the females. Pearl danios prefer to live in shoals. In the wild, they have a great many predators and if attacked they all disperse in different directions to create confusion and avoid being eaten. The water temperature should be about 75°F and the tank should be brightly lit and well planted. Although pearl danios originate from soft water areas, they are one of the few cyprinids that will spawn in hard water. Set up an aquarium with a bunch of plants at one end and feed the prospective pair well for a few days before placing them in the breeding aquarium and raising the temperature slowly until it reaches about 79°F. The spawning should take place during the next morning, particularly if the tank receives some direct sunlight. The pair do a lot of chasing and spiraling through the plants, where the eggs are released and fertilized. Once the spawning is over, remove the parents or they will eat the eggs. The eggs hatch some time the following day, depending on the temperature of the tank, and the fry will be free-swimming some four or five days later. At this stage you can begin to feed them on a liquid fry food.

Above: *At 4in the giant danio (Danio malabaricus) is much larger than the pearl and zebra danios. It has the same requirements with regard to water, breeding and feeding, but its foods need not be chopped so small. The body is slightly deeper with a more pointed snout; the females tend to be plumper and less colorful than the male fishes.*

Left: *The white cloud mountain minnow (Tanichthys albonubes) is another of the really easy-care danios. It will thrive in hard or soft water, with a temperature on the low side - about 72°F is warm enough. Flake food is ideal, along with frozen Tubifex or Daphnia. As it only grows to 1.6in at most, you can offer it newly hatched brineshrimp, even when adult.*

Right: *The harlequinfish, or harlequin rasbora, (Rasbora heteromorpha) is`a small, peaceful fish, often seen in tropical aquariums. It is quite deep towards the front of the body around the belly, but tapers to a very narrow tail. All the fins are clear and the body has a lovely pinkish-blue hue. The rear half of the body is distinguished by a black marking that follows the body shape. These beautiful little community fish only grow to about 1.6in and do best when kept in a shoal. They make good tankmates for danios and livebearers and thrive in the same conditions. Harlequins eat flake, live or freeze-dried foods, such as Daphnia or brineshrimp. They do not spawn as readily as danios and will need soft acidic water in the aquarium for breeding to be successful.*

Sharks

Although these fish are often referred to as sharks, there is no chance of losing an arm or a leg to any of them! The word shark has become assigned to them because they have a very active and similar swimming pattern to the marine terror. These sharks are relatively peaceful, although they can chase the odd tank occupant about a little. Other fishes may find their activity disruptive.

Below: The red-tailed black sharks (Labeo bicolor) *from Thailand are probably the most popular of the sharks. Red-tailed sharks are best kept in small shoals and prefer warm water of about 78°F. They eat most dried foods, but relish live food, such as Daphnia and bloodworm. Provide a food that sinks for these very active, bottom- to middle-water dwelling fish. They can grow as large as 7in; a 36in tank will suffice when the fish is juvenile, but adults need a 48in tank. This fish is a jumper, so keep the tank covered at all times.*

Above: *Slim and horizontally compressed, the Bala, or silver shark, (Balantiocheilus melanopterus) is one of the largest sharks, growing to 8-9in. These very active fish need a tank measuring at least 36in long. The water temperature should be about 75°F, but otherwise the water composition is unimportant. Offer the fish a varied diet, including flake food, freeze-dried Tubifex and live foods, such as chopped earthworms. Like most sharks, this species is a jumper, so keep the tank well covered with fairly thick, heavy glass that cannot be dislodged.*

Right: *The red-finned shark (Labeo erythrurus) is a close cousin of the red-tailed black shark and also stems from Asia. The body shape is virtually the same, except that this species is slightly more slender than its cousin. The body color is a deep gray and all the fins are orange or red. This fish grows to about 6in or perhaps a little more, and requires the same care and feeding as the red-tailed black shark. This is the most notorious jumper of all the sharks and can be a bit of a bully towards the other fish around it if they are not up to returning a blow now and again.*

Loaches

Loaches are a small group of scavengers that make up the Cobitidae family of fishes. They are very active, nocturnal bottom-dwellers. The botias and some cobitids possess a spine in front of the eye that they can raise to inflict considerable damage on other fishes or on the unwary aquarist. Most loaches seen in aquariums are from Southeast Asia, where they live in muddy, oxygen-depleted waters. They gulp air at the surface and absorb oxygen in the gut lining to compensate.

Below: The orange-finned botia (Botia modesta) is identical in care and feeding requirements to the clown loach (see page 51). It does not grow quite as large, 5in being an excellent size. This is a peaceful little bottom-dweller, an undemanding tank occupant and an ideal scavenger. It chases greedily after all foods and as soon as it is meal time these fish seem to be charged with life. The water temperature should be about 79°F, but otherwise the water composition is relatively unimportant.

Right: The weather loach (Misgurnus anguillicaudatus) comes from Asia - from Siberia, China, Korea through to Japan. Although the gold form is shown here, the normal coloration is a light brown background with dark brown blotches, giving the fish a mottled appearance. The common name derives from the fish's alleged sensitivity to changes in air pressure. It becomes particularly active just before and during periods of thundery weather. It tolerates water kept at 68-75°F.

Below: The clown loach (Botia macracantha) *takes its name from the gaudy colors, which look like a clown's costume. The base color is flesh pink overlaid with three black vertical bands - one through the eye, one just in front of the dorsal fin and one just after. Added to this, the dorsal and anal fins are black, while the remaining fins are orange. Clown loaches, like most* Botia *sp., are quite timid, but this wears off to a degree after some time in the same aquarium, although they never become aggressive. These fish love a fast-flowing current in the aquarium, somewhere where they can swim head-on into the flow and exercise their muscles. A fairly warm tank of about 79°F will make clown loaches feel very much at home. They relish live foods and will gobble up chopped earthworms and* Daphnia *as soon as they hit the bottom. Like all* Botia *sp., they are bottom-dwellers and feed both day and night by scavenging with their little feelers. Clown loaches can grow quite large, reaching 8in in a large aquarium, but they normally attain about 5in. These are shoaling fish in the wild, so keep them in small groups. Newly imported specimens can be difficult to acclimatize to aquarium conditions.*

Other loaches of interest

The zebra loach (*Botia striata*) is a delightful, peaceful little fish that grows to a maximum of 4in. The body shape resembles that of the clown loach, but is slightly longer and slimmer, and the color is cream overlaid with many closely spaced olive to dark green bars. As with most *Botia* sp., they are best kept in small groups and often scurry around together in the aquarium. After an initial day to settle in, they are soon 'out and about' and not at all timid. They prefer a temperature of about 79°F and water that is very clean and slightly alkaline, but they are quite adaptable and will thrive in many different water compositions. Provide live foods if possible, but these fish also relish dried foods. The most important thing is that the food sinks quickly, as zebra loaches are bottom-feeders.

Catfishes

Many of the popular tropical aquarium catfishes originate from South and Central America, Africa and Asia. Most are rather drably colored, mainly because they need good camouflage to avoid predation. As they usually frequent the bottom, the ideal colors are brown and black. Many have poor sight, as they are often nocturnal or live in silt-laden waters. To compensate for this, catfishes have developed barbels, which are covered in taste receptors. Barbels may be long and used for hunting, as in the pimelodids or, as in the *Corydoras* catfishes, short and used to burrow and tease their way into the gravel to detect food or insects. Some catfishes scavenge at the bottom for tasty morsels, others are midwater swimmers that feed mainly on insect larvae. Large predatory species hunt for small live fish, a few feed on fruit and seeds and some of the most bizarre species are parasitic - even to the extent of feeding on other catfishes.

Some of these 'cats' have developed large, rubbery, sucker-type mouths with which they remove the algae and any other protein-rich coatings that cover plants, rocks or gravel. Some catfish species cover great distances, both in daylight and during the hours of darkness. They may be specialist feeders, whereas the catfishes that remain hidden in a cave for most of the time will tend to feed on virtually anything, because they have to take what they can, rather than hunt for a particular food. Many catfish species are quite capable of eating very large fish or other large aquatic creatures. All in all, they represent a very mixed and fascinating

Above: Jordan's catfish (Arius jordani) *is a shoaling fish from the coast of Peru. Only young specimens are suitable for the aquarium. Keep them in groups in brackish water.*

group. It is a good idea to have at least one catfish in every aquarium, as they tend to clear up and eat any waste or leftovers that other fish ignore. Do not look on them just as scavengers, however; they are interesting fish in their own right and appreciate proper feeding, rather than living off the scraps left by other fishes in the community aquarium.

Corydoras catfishes

Of all the tropical aquarium catfishes, *Corydoras* catfishes must be the most popular. There are many types of *Corydoras*, a group of very small, well-armored catfishes from South America, with a variety of color patterns depending on their native habitat. If at all possible, set up the aquarium to simulate the slow-moving rivers of South America, where these catfishes come from. Introduce plenty of plants, some bogwood and fine gravel to make them feel at home. A tank containing only *Corydoras* catfishes does not make a very good community, as the fish tend to spend most of the time at the bottom of the tank, leaving the top half looking empty. *Corydoras* catfishes often take gasps of air from the atmosphere, so do not be alarmed if your fish make a sudden split-second dash from the bottom to the surface; this behavior is totally normal. These busy little beavers are seen in nearly every home community tank and most are easy to keep, although a few can be quite delicate. They prefer their water to be slightly cooler than most other tropicals but will quite happily live at the optimum temperature of 75°F. However, some species need very specific water conditions, especially if they are wild-caught fish, so check before buying.

Although most *Corydoras* catfishes are visible during the daylight hours, many are more active after dark. 'Corries', as they are often affectionately known, will eat most foods, retrieving anything dropped by the other fishes in the tank, but as they are bottom-dwellers they need a food that sinks to the bottom. They relish small chopped earthworms, soaked pellets or waterlogged flake, and finely blended beef heart or raw fish. *Corydoras* will breed in the home aquarium, although some species are easier than others. They are best bred in an aquarium of their own, with two males and one female. The female is pestered by the two males and lays her eggs on the plants and glass. The males then fertilize the eggs, which hatch after three or four days or so and fall to the bottom. There they live off a yolk sac for a few more days and then you can feed them on fine fry foods or newly hatched brineshrimp.

Right: The distinctive Corydoras robineae *from the Rio Negro is easily identified by the stripes on the caudal fin. It prefers slightly soft, acidic water and a planted aquarium with a fine substrate so that it does not damage its delicate barbels when feeding. Small, live invertebrates, such as* Daphnia, *form an important part of its natural diet and if fed these, the fish develops an iridescent sheen - a sign of good health. Alternatives are frozen or flake foods. It grows to 3in and a shoal is a welcome addition to a community tank.*

Above: The aeneus, *or bronze, catfish* (Corydoras aeneus) *has quite a bit of metallic green coloration as well and is probably one of the most common miniature aquarium catfish. Like all* Corydoras sp., *this one has rows of plated scales along each flank for protection against predators. The fins are equipped with spines and the mouth has barbels for rooting through gravel in search of food. Bronze catfishes are completely peaceful and probably best kept in groups of three or more. Even in a mixed community, males often follow the females about. Males are usually smaller and less robust than females.*

Below: Hoplosternum thoracatum, *occasionally called port hoplo or atipa, has two rows of plates on the body. It belongs to the same family as the* Corydoras *catfishes, but is much larger. H. thoracatum is an ideal, peaceful scavenger in a community of larger fish. It prefers hard, slightly alkaline water, but will do quite well in almost any conditions. It can be bred in the aquarium, where the male builds a nest of bubbles at the surface and anchors it to the side of the tank among floating material. Make sure there is the minimum of surface movement or the nest will break up. The pair place their eggs in the bubblenest, where they are guarded by the male. The fry live off their large yolk sacs for the first two or three days and can then be fed with newly hatched brineshrimps. H. thoracatum is often mistaken for* Callichthys callichthys, *but that particular fish has a rounded caudal fin.*

Above: The peppered corydoras (Corydoras paleatus) *is peaceful and a good little community fish. It is brown with a slightly purple tinge and a number of black blotches over the body. Peppered catfishes prefer quite cool conditions - about 72°F - but tolerate temperatures anywhere within 3°F of this. When females of this species are ripe with eggs they become really plump. This is probably the commonest of all the available* Corydoras *catfishes and one of the easiest to breed in the aquarium. Myers' catfish* (Corydoras myersi) *is another of the more common* Corydoras. *It is one of the hardier species and makes a welcome addition to any peaceful community aquarium. Myers' catfish has a light buff body color and is one of the largest* Corydoras *species, growing to 3in.*

Suckermouth and whiptail catfishes

There are many different forms of suckermouth catfishes, with a great deal of variety in shape and size. 'Common plecos' is the catch-all name for most of the common suckermouth fish offered for sale. The name comes from the second part of the scientific name *Hypostomus plecostomus*, a particular species that is probably hardly ever available. Most owners lump together their fish with the name 'pleco', usually with a prefix such as 'clown' pleco or 'blue-eyed' pleco. Suckermouth catfishes play an important role in the aquarium. Whereas most other catfishes scavenge on food left behind by other fish, suckermouths will search all over the tank for certain algae as a food source and thus keep the tank partially free of this often unwanted plant growth. However, there may not be enough algal growth to meet their needs, so supplement their diet with peas and lettuce. Most of these catfishes eat all the usual aquarium foods, but can only manage very small particles and tend to suck up rather than chew any food that is put in the tank for them. Many suckermouth catfishes are nocturnal, hiding behind plants or under rocks during the day, but most will

Below: Common plecos (Hypostomus sp.) have large rubbery lips on the underside for sucking food and algae off the rocks and glass. These territorial fish may grow to 10in or even more.

Above: Quite a few types of bristlenose plecos (Ancistrus sp.) are offered for sale. These non-aggressive fish remain quite small. Males are distinguished by the many fleshy bristles all over the front of the head. In females, shorter bristles fringe the snout. Body colors and markings vary between individual species, some being brown, many being black. Bristlenoses make excellent algae cleaners; if there are no plants in the tank feed them peas or blanched lettuce. Bristlenoses are happiest in moderately hard water with a neutral pH level and a temperature of about 75°F.

Left: Hypostomus sp. have three rows of plates along their flanks, covered in very fine dermal denticles, which make the surface feel like sandpaper. They have quite a large dorsal and forked tail and a pair of very small eyes right on top of the head. They are quite timid and may hide if the tank is too brightly lit, but will live happily in most safe temperature and water conditions. If two of these fish are kept together in the same tank they may bicker a little, but rarely do one another harm. Apart from the algae in the tank, they also eat green food, such as lettuce and spinach.

make an appearance in daylight hours, especially if food is placed in the tank. Nevertheless, it is a good idea to drop some food in the tank for them just before the lights go out at night, but make sure that it will sink; like most catfishes, suckermouths are usually bottom-dwellers. Whiptails require well-filtered, mature water that is high in oxygen. If the oxygen content of the water is severely depleted, these fish will rise to the surface for atmospheric air, which they are able to absorb through the hind gut. They are highly intolerant of aquarium medications containing methylene blue and have been known to jump from the water to escape such treatments.

Right: There are many types of farlowella catfishes (Farlowella gracilis), but most are very much alike. The stick catfish, as it is also called, is quite armored, with a pointed, slightly upturned snout. It prefers temperatures of 75°F and is quite easy to keep, but dislikes many of the standard aquarium disease remedies, so take special care when adding chemicals to the water.

Left: An exceptionally beautiful catfish, Panaque nigrolineatus, *can be very difficult to acclimatize to aquarium conditions. Check that fish do not have sunken eyes or very hollow bellies when you buy them, Provide clean, well-filtered, highly oxygenated water in a planted aquarium. Offer newly acquired specimens green foods, as their digestive system seems unable to cope with high-protein foods at this time. They may browse on aquarium plants. Once acclimatized, you can add chopped prawns to their diet. P. nigrolineatus can be territorial towards its own kind. It can grow quite large - up to 18in.*

*Left: As its name suggests, the sailfin pleco (*Pterygoplichthys gibbiceps) *has a very large dorsal fin. Its body is covered in round black spots that are usually bolder in juvenile fish. The bright copper base color may also fade with age. This fish can grow to about 16in in a large tank. Sailfins feed predominantly on green foods and usually confine their aggressive tendencies to chasing other fish away from tasty morsels. They prefer slightly hard, alkaline water at 75°F.*

Below: Most dwarf plecos belong to the Peckoltia *genus, a group of quite decorative, small suckermouths that never grow much more than 3in long. Like the clown pleco (P. vittata) shown here, they are superb little algae cleaners and very peaceful, only becoming argumentative if another fish tries to muscle in on their hiding places, which they guard quite fiercely for their size.* Peckoltia *like to hide during the daytime and come out to feed at night, so you may not see them too often.*

*Above: The royal farlowella (*Sturisoma panamense) *is plain brown with darker brown flanks. It has a very high dorsal fin and usually two whips on the tail. These ray extensions grow much longer with age and may coil like springs. Like most suckermouth catfishes, S. panamense is quite armor-plated for protection. It lives happily in a range of waters from soft to hard, but changes from one to the other should be gradual. Do not introduce* Sturisoma *to newly set-up tanks, as they prefer mature conditions. These fish may breed in the aquarium. Males have cheek bristles. There are several other species of* Sturisoma, *but S. panamense is probably the most commonly available.*

Pimelodus and *pimelodella* catfishes

'Pim' is the abbreviation often used to describe the many species of catfishes in the *Pimelodus* and *Pimelodella* groupings from South and Central America. Some are quite predatory, while others live on aquatic creatures and the fry of other fishes. Happily, most of them will thrive on all the standard aquarium foods, although some of the larger species do require something more substantial.

Right: The angelicus catfish (Pimelodus pictus) *grows to about 5in and is more active during the day than most other pims. It appreciates some live food in its diet, so do not put it with small fish that could become a meal. The* angelicus catfish *is quite happy in hard water, although it seems to prefer soft, slightly acidic conditions. Apart from its piscivorous appetite, it is quite peaceful and a good community catfish if kept with suitably sized tankmates.*

Synodontis catfishes

Synodontis are a group of catfishes from Africa. Many are natives of the great African lakes, Lake Tanganyika and Lake Malawi. They are very active fishes, but most are nocturnal. Many *Synodontis* are insectivorous but usually accept flake foods, very small pieces of meat and, naturally, aquatic invertebrates. *Synodontis* are also partial to garden peas and will often race out of their cave to feed on them. Of the many *Synodontis* species, about five spend more than 50 percent of their time swimming upside-down. *Synodontis* catfishes usually do well in the average aquarium and species from the Rift Lakes make good companions for the African Rift Lake cichlids.

Below: The stunning Synodontis angelicus *has a black body completely overlaid with white dots. Cheaper specimens lack the strong black color. The striped fins are transparent in places. Color varies between fishes; some have many spots, others have white bars and spots. S. angelicus is happy in most types of water at about 77°F. In a good-sized tank, it can grow to 8in.*

Right: The upside-down catfish (Synodontis nigriventris) *spends much of its time swimming inverted near the water surface. The belly of the fish is darker than its back, thus S. nigriventris is afforded greater protection from predators. Upside-down catfishes grow to a maximum length of 4in. They have quite long 'whiskers', and the tail and dorsal fin are pointed, making them look squared-off in shape.*

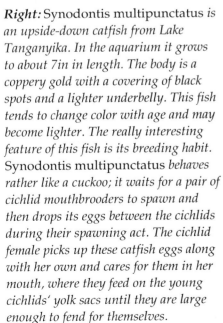

Above: Synodontis flavitaeniatus *comes from the Zaire River and pools. It is one of the smaller Synodontis species, with exceptional specimens growing to a maximum of 8in. It is a strikingly colored fish; the golden-yellow bars seen in healthy* young specimens make it a popular choice. Feeding this long-lived species is simple, as the fish avidly consumes most small frozen and dried foods, as well as flakes and pellets. It benefits from the addition of small live foods, such as Daphnia and Mysis shrimp.

Right: Synodontis multipunctatus *is an upside-down catfish from Lake Tanganyika. In the aquarium it grows to about 7in in length. The body is a coppery gold with a covering of black spots and a lighter underbelly. This fish tends to change color with age and may become lighter. The really interesting feature of this fish is its breeding habit. Synodontis multipunctatus behaves rather like a cuckoo; it waits for a pair of cichlid mouthbrooders to spawn and then drops its eggs between the cichlids during their spawning act. The cichlid female picks up these catfish eggs along with her own and cares for them in her mouth, where they feed on the young cichlids' yolk sacs until they are large enough to fend for themselves.*

Giant catfishes

With the advent of modern tank building techniques and very strong adhesives, it is no longer a problem to build large tanks. Aquariums measuring 72in long with a capacity of 180 gallons are quite common throughout the hobby. This means that the scope for keeping larger species of tropical fish is greater than ever before. Many of these fishes are given a 'pet' status by their owners, and when kept on their own they tend to develop a personality that is theirs alone. Due to their large size, it is not usually possible to decorate the tank with plants or any quantity of rockwork, as the fish soon demolish these with disastrous results! Most pet tanks are furnished with just the basics, such as gravel and an undergravel filter, coupled with a power filter to cope with the large volume of waste that these fish inevitably produce.

Right: The striped shovelnose catfish (Sorubim lima) is the most commonly seen of the catfish giants, and juveniles are often offered for sale at 4-5in. However, with good care and careful feeding they can be expected to reach at least 15in in length. Striped shovelnoses are very long slim fish, with a flat head. The top half of the body is brown, the lower part white, with black flanks in between. The eyes are set back on the head behind the huge jaw, which gives it the look of an alligator. These fish also have a large forked tail and long feelers around the mouth. Striped shovelnose catfishes favor medium-hard, very slightly alkaline water kept at a temperature of about 77°F. Obviously, you must keep this highly predatory fish away from any other fish that might slip into its huge mouth. Suitable foods are easy to find and you should feed the fish about three times each week. Raw fish is a good base food and can include whitebait, lancefish and any runts or deformities that your dealer can supply. Beef heart and pellets are accepted, but are not as ideal a food as fish.

King of the catfishes

Redtailed catfish (*Phractocephalus hemioliopterus*) can grow to over 36in long and have earned something of a cult following. The top of the body is slate gray to black, the underside is white, sometimes with a dark vertical band. The light gray head has a profusion of black spots. The tail is red and there may be some orange around the edge of the dorsal fin. Coupled with its long white barbels and large mouth, it is an impressive fish and can command a high price. Clearly, it requires a large tank with efficient filtration to take away all the mess that the fish creates. Aquarium decorations will be demolished, so confine the furnishing to gravel. Large catfishes can deliver a nasty bite to the hand that feeds them.

Above: Perrunichthys perruno is brown and covered in dark gray to black spots, with a white underside. It has a large dorsal fin and a forked tail. Like the shovelnoses, this fish can be quite lethargic and only active when hungry, so avoid the temptation to feed it too heavily. It is not as mean as the shovels, but can still swallow its share of small fish. Provide medium-hard, slightly alkaline water at a temperature of 77°F and carry out regular large partial water changes. P. perruno is a good tankmate for the striped shovelnoses when kept in a sufficiently large tank.

Below: With the tiger shovelnose (Pseudoplatystoma fasciatus), *we come to the real predators. The body is covered with black stripes, hence the common name. All the unpaired fins have black spots rather than stripes. Certain specimens can grow to as much as 30in or more! At this size,* P. fasciatus *needs a really large, well-covered tank, but in a home aquarium its maximum length is usually nearer 24in. Be sure to provide it with adequate space, as this fish takes fright easily and may damage its snout.*

Killifishes

Killifishes, or egglaying toothcarps as they are sometimes described, are a very colorful group of usually small, elongated fishes. Most come from Africa, but some are found in the Americas, Asia and Europe. Unfortunately, they do not make very good community fish and are certainly not the best choice for beginners. Killifish usually come from very soft-water regions, which also tend to be acidic in composition, although a few are found in more alkaline and harder water areas. The fish often live in shaded areas of rainforest, trapped in small pools, where water temperatures may fall as low as 70°F or lower. If you wish to keep killifishes in an aquarium, you must provide the appropriate water conditions, otherwise they are unlikely to survive for very long. This being so and because most other species (apart from some tetras and a few others) do not really thrive in such conditions, it is easy to see why killifishes are usually kept only with their own kind.

Another problem is that they are naturally shortlived. Some species may live for less than a year in the wild, so if these fish are kept in poor conditions, their lifespan can be shortened dramatically, all of which could be disheartening for someone who is keeping aquarium fishes for the first time.

In the right conditions, these fish can be easy to breed. In their natural habitat, many killifishes live in small pools, puddles and streams that evaporate in the dry season. To avoid total extinction, the fish have evolved a very clever strategy. Throughout the breeding season, some killifishes spread their eggs on plant matter, while others bury their eggs in peat. When the water evaporates, the eggs - protected in the slightly damp material - become dormant and enter a state of suspended animation. After a few months, the rains

return and once the eggs come into contact with water, they become active again and hatch. Only a few hatch at first, just in case the water is just a shower and the pools do not refill, but gradually most of the eggs hatch out. This is why some killifishes only live for a year; since they may be trapped in pools that dry out every year, they only require a lifespan of one year.

It is usually possible to distinguish the sex of killifishes, as males are more colorful and have more splendid fins. As in many species of fishes, males are often rather aggressive towards other males and it is not a good idea to keep more than one male of any given species in a tank. Indeed, during the breeding season, males can be aggressive towards females, so keep two females to one male. Given their short lifespan and specialized water requirements, killifishes are not often seen in aquarium shops, nor are they commonly kept.

Left: *The colorful Playfair's panchax (Pachypanchax playfairi) only grows to about 3in, with females being slightly smaller. The body color is made up of rows of orange spots with rows of greenish blue in between, and these colors are also present in the fins. The female's fins are usually clear, apart from the dorsal fin, which has a black blotch at the base. Males can be very aggressive during breeding time, so avoid keeping more than one male in the aquarium. Feed these killifishes with small live foods if possible, otherwise use frozen or freeze-dried foods. The water temperature should be about 72°F, but this is one killifish that does not demand soft-water conditions.*

Above: *The American flagfish (Jordanella floridae) from Florida in North America can only be regarded as semi-tropical. In captivity, it will accept a temperature as low as 66°F or even lower, but it is happiest at 72°F and does quite well in hard water. Its coloration is quite variable, with rows of spots running along the flanks that can be anything from bright red to orange or nearly yellow. The middle of the body has a black blotch. Females are less colorful, with a dark blotch towards the rear of the body. The American flagfish has vegetarian tastes and will nibble at algae growth and plants in the aquarium. Plastic plants may survive its attentions better than real plants.*

Other killifishes of interest

The black-finned pearlfish (*Cynolebias nigripinnis*) has a beautiful light blue body, overlaid with white to pearly-cream spots. As in many killies, the dorsal fin is set quite a long way back on the body and the anal fin is very long. Females are basically the same shape, but usually plumper and much less colorful. Males will reach about 2in, females slightly less. Avoid keeping two males together in breeding condition to minimize the high degree of aggression often associated with male killifishes. Provide soft, acidic water and maintain it at about 72°F. Like most killifishes, black-finned pearlfishes enjoy a diet of small live foods, such as chopped worms, and freeze-dried or frozen foods. The Argentine pearlfish (*Cynolebias bellottii*) is a slightly larger version of the black-finned pearlfish, the male growing to about 3in in length. Its water and feeding requirements are the same as that of its cousin.

Livebearers

Of all the available tropical aquarium fishes, none are better to start with than livebearers. Livebearers are hardy, very active, easy to maintain and easy to induce into breeding in the aquarium; in fact, it is more difficult to stop them from breeding! Livebearers are usually peaceful and an excellent addition to any gentle community aquarium. So what is a livebearer? Well, all the fish that we have discussed so far are egglayers, i.e. fish that lay eggs and then fertilize them outside the female's body. In livebearers, the eggs are retained within the female's body after fertilization and the embryos develop for about one month before being released. When the fry are released, they are usually exact miniature replicas of the female. In some species this process can be repeated every two months and newcomers to the hobby are usually fascinated by it; even experienced tropical fish hobbyists continue to be amazed at the emergence of the fry.

All male livebearers have a gonopodium, a modified anal fin used by the male to spray his sperm at the female's vent to fertilize the eggs. He does this by swimming around and pestering her until he can get alongside her. The male then contorts his gonopodium into a forward-facing position to fertilize the eggs inside the female. After four or five weeks, the female will be ready to release her young. She develops a 'gravid spot', a dark, swollen area on the lower part of the abdomen, just in front of the anal fin. She will try to release the young in a quiet spot near a clump of plants and, although they hide in the vegetation, other fish - even their parents - regard them as food. You can protect the fry by using a breeding trap - see page 67.

Above: A marbled form of the black molly (Poecilia sp.). *It has a large dorsal fin and a round tail and grows to about 3in excluding the tail. Mollies eat most flake foods, especially vegetable flake. They also relish freeze-dried* Daphnia, *bloodworm and brineshrimp and are particularly fond of these foods if fed to them live. It is also a good idea to offer some vegetable matter, such as garden peas with the skins removed or* small pieces of cooked broad beans. Black mollies prefer temperatures of 79°F - higher than normal for community tropicals. Like their close relative the guppy, these fish are easy to breed but can be a little nervous, which may lead to miscarriages. They are best bred in a tank of their own, where they produce broods of 10-40 fry. There is an aquarium-bred strain of the black molly with a forked tail, known as the lyretail.

Mollies

In the wild, mollies are usually found in quite hard water areas and river estuaries, so it is a good idea to add one teaspoon of sea salt to every 3 gallons of tank water. Black mollies also like some plants in the tank to give them cover and to nibble at. If you do decide to add salt to the tank, make sure that other fish and any plants can withstand the brackish conditions, or use plastic plants.

The black molly (*Poecilia* sp.) is something of an unknown quantity in that it is a hybrid and nobody seems to know from which two species it was bred. This fish breeds true to coloration and produces viable young, which should not be the case with a hybrid. There are also marbled, albino and green forms.

Guppies

The guppy must be one of the best-known tropical aquarium fishes, as well as one of the most beautiful and prolific. It is not aggressive to any degree and can be kept with any other fish that will not be aggressive towards it or grow big enough to eat it. Guppies make no special demands regarding care and will survive in less than perfect conditions (although this is no excuse to neglect them). The guppy originates from Central America and the northern part of South America. In its natural state, it is a relatively uninteresting fish with very little coloration, but over the years, fish breeders have developed various highly colored strains and forms with greatly elaborated fins. This breeding work has been concentrated on the male fishes, which even in the relatively drab wild specimens show more color than the females. Depending on the particular aquarium-bred strain, the dorsal fin may either be small or

Below: A pair of green variegated delta tail guppies (Poecilia reticulata). The lower fish is a male with a splendid tail, but even the female fish - normally drab compared to the male - has benefited from the breeding program and now sports a strikingly colored tail. The name 'guppy' comes from the naturalist Robert Guppy, who first collected the fishes in Trinidad during the 1860s.

Right: The sailfin molly (Poecilia velifera) is found in Central America, Mexico and around Florida and Texas (possibly partly due to introduction by man). It is light green with many lighter pink scales over the whole body, these colors extending into all the fins. Males of this species (the upper fish here) have a large dorsal fin, as high as or even higher than the body itself.

massively flowing, but the male's tail will always be like a long flowing scarf. The tail may be one of several different shapes, depending on the breed, and will also have various names, such as 'delta tail', 'veiltail' or 'fantail', and so on. The colors of these fish are absolutely stunning. Again, depending on the particular strain of guppy, it may be red, blue, green, black or any combination of these and any other colors, too. The colors may extend across the body right up to the head. Females are far less colorful but larger, growing to about 2in, whereas the male only reaches about 1.4in in body length, which could lead you to think that these are two totally different fish. Guppies like their tanks to be quite warm - 78°F is about right. They also like the water to be quite hard and alkaline, never soft and acidic. Guppies eat all manner of foods, including flake, freeze-dried brineshrimps, *Daphnia*, bloodworm and most frozen foods. They appreciate vegetable matter, such as canned garden peas or blanched lettuce.

Platies

The platy is another common livebearer from Mexico and other parts of Central America. Male fishes grow to a maximum of 2in and have a pointed anal fin, whereas females are often a little larger, with a rounded anal fin. These quite plump fish have slightly upturned little mouths for feeding from the surface. The

Right: In the platy (Xiphophorus maculatus), red, orange, yellow and black are the predominant colors, although other colors are often seen in aquarium-bred stock. Platies are easy to sex, as the male (upper fish) has a pointed anal fin whereas the female's anal fin is rounded. Females also tend to be plumper than males. The platy is always ready to breed and females are rarely unfertilized. A mature female can release up to 100 young at a time, but 40 is nearer the normal brood size. These plump little fish do best in mildly hard water at 75°F.

dorsal fin and tail are very rounded. Tank-bred fishes often bear little resemblance in color to their wild counterparts. In the absence of members of the opposite sex of their own type, platies and swordtails will crossbreed. Try to prevent this if at all possible.

Swordtails

The swordtail is very much like the platy, but in males the bottom ray of the caudal fin extends to a very long point, like the blade of a sword. As in the platies, there are many color variants of this species, some with extra long dorsal fins and anal fins, too. When buying a male swordtail, check that its anal fin has not developed in this way, as it will have trouble spawning with females. Swordtails prefer slightly alkaline, medium-hard water at 77°F.

Using a breeding trap

To avoid the young being eaten, you can float a breeding trap in the main aquarium. This is usually a net frame or a clear miniature plastic aquarium about 4-5in square with a small mesh grid in the bottom. When the female is nearly ready to drop her young, place her in the trap above the grid. As she releases the young, they fall through the grid and out of harm's way. As she does not tend the young, the female can be returned to the main aquarium after a little rest. Raise the fry in the breeding trap on finely crushed flake until they are big enough not to be eaten or, better still, place them in another aquarium to grow to a safe size before releasing them into the community tank. Females can store sperm from a male and use it to fertilize up to five or six future batches of eggs, so it is quite possible to have a female and no male and still have several broods of young guppies. Male guppies are very attentive towards females, so it is a good idea to buy two or three females for every male or else the female may become worn out.

Young females may produce as few as three or four fry, but older guppies may - and often do - drop more than 100 fry at a go. Separate males from females as soon as possible if you do not want a guppy plague on your hands!

Above: Rainbow wagtail platies (Xiphophorus variatus) *with a male fish at bottom. This species only differs from Xiphophorus maculatus in that it is slimmer. Many of the platies for sale today are crossbreeds of the two species and it may be that the two fishes are one species. Platies are often given names to match their color pattern, such as 'sunset platy' or 'tuxedo platy'.*

Right: Excluding the long tail that the male develops as it matures, the swordtail (Xiphophorus helleri) *will grow to about 3in long, sometimes a little more. Swordtails relish live foods, such as* Daphnia *and bloodworm, but will do very well on flake and freeze-dried foods, and frozen foods, such as* Tubifex. *They also appreciate some vegetable matter in their diet.*

Cichlids

Cichlids are an amazingly diverse group of fishes that almost form a complete hobby on their own. Most of them come from South and Central America and Africa, with a couple of species from Asia. The smallest species only grow to 2in, whereas the largest reach over 24in. Some are highly colorful, whereas others are quite drab. Some cichlids are flat and laterally 'squashed' in shape, while others are cylindrical. Certain species are completely peaceful, whereas others are the most aggressive, ill-tempered fish that we know. All cichlids are territorial, some more so than others. Most are relatively easy to breed and this is where their true attraction lies, for they look after their young with the greatest care and devotion.

In the past, most cichlids were regarded as difficult to keep, due to their aggression and size and, indeed, some are specialist fish. Today, however, with larger tanks and a greater knowledge of their needs, even novice aquarists can keep cichlids with great success.

American and African dwarf cichlids

The term 'dwarf' cichlid is a loose one, generally applied to cichlids that are 3in or less in length. Some people would regard a 4in cichlid as a dwarf, whereas others would say 2in is the maximum for a dwarf. Dwarf cichlids are found in the Americas and Africa. Most of them can be kept in an aquarium with a capacity of 7 gallons, although a tank twice this size is far better. All dwarf cichlids can be

Breeding dwarf cichlids

When a pair is ready to spawn, both fish select a rock and peck it clean. An egg tube, or ovipositor, starts to protrude from the female's underside and eventually she lays her eggs on the rock and the male fertilizes them. They lay a total of 100-200 and once all the eggs are laid, the female takes up position fanning them with her fins and pecking them clean. Both parents guard the eggs from all other fish, attacking potential predators if approached. The eggs hatch after about three days and the parents take them to a hole that they have dug in the gravel. Here they are guarded for another week until they can swim for themselves. At this stage, the whole family go out and about together to find food, which you should supply in the form of newly hatched brineshrimps.

aggressive, but only in the pursuit of establishing a piece of territory in which to breed and raise their young unmolested.

In the early 1970s, cichlids began to be exported for the aquarium hobby from the two great Rift Lakes in Africa, namely Lake Malawi and Lake Tanganyika. From Lake Tanganyika came a group of fishes that generally remained quite small - the *Lamprologus* species and one or two others. These fish can be kept in a community tank together with other Lake Tanganyikan fishes or in species tanks containing a group of the same species. They do not mix well with other types of fish due to their highly aggressive behavior and territorial nature.

The Rift Lakes of Africa have very hard, clean water and you must provide first-class water quality in the aquarium if the fish are to remain in good condition and breed. For the best results, provide well-filtered water with a total hardness of 15-20°dH (see page 29) and a temperature of 78°F.

Right: The cockatoo dwarf cichlid (Apistogramma cacatuoides) *from the Amazon may fly out from its territory to chase off intruders, but is generally peaceful and makes a good introduction to 'dwarfs'. The first few rays of the dorsal fin stick up like a head-dress, but the body colors are not as startling as in some 'Apistos'. Females are banana yellow with a black band through the eye and a smaller head-dress. Like most American dwarfs, they enjoy live foods but eat dried and flake foods. Provide warm water; 79°F is ideal. This fish spawns in the same way as other dwarfs, but likes half a coconut shell on its side or a broken clay flowerpot as a spawning site.*

Below: The ram, or butterfly, cichlid (Microgeophagus ramirezi) from South America is only about 2in long. Ramirez's dwarf cichlid, as it is also known, is quite timid, but if kept with other small, non-aggressive fish in a well-planted tank it soon ventures out.

Rams prefer soft water but will live in hard water, as long as it is clean and maintained at 79°F. Buy fish that are full in the body and active swimmers. Rams eat most foods, but should be offered live food at least once a week for good health.

Above: The krib, or kribensis, (Pelvicachromis pulcher) needs plants and caves for cover and clean, very warm water. It breeds like other dwarf cichlids, placing its eggs under a cave or flowerpot. Before spawning, the *female develops a very plump, rosy pink belly. While breeding and defending its spawning site and young, this fish can become highly aggressive. At other times it is a good community fish, provided its tankmates are quite hardy.*

Right: The delightful little brichardi, or Princess of Burundi, cichlids (Lamprologus brichardi) only grow to 4in. They breed in gregarious little groups in a tank measuring at least 39in long, with plenty of rocks to form territories and spawning sites and hard, alkaline water at about 78°F. When a pair spawn, the rest of the brichardi cichlids in the community help guard the young. As the young grow, the larger fish breed again and the young help to look after the next clutch of eggs and fry, and thus a whole community of caring fishes develops. Before spawning, the group digs a huge pit with their mouths; since this may undermine the rockwork, do make sure it is sturdy.

Rift Lake cichlids

The cichlids from Lake Malawi and Lake Tanganyika in Africa are very colorful, highly aggressive, hardy, easy to breed and make a superb display. They require a good undergravel filtration system, as they are very intolerant of nitrite and soon react adversely if any waste matter is allowed to build up in the tank. These fish tend to dig into the gravel and excavate down to the undergravel filter plate, unless there is a gravel tidy to prevent this. Rift Lake cichlids need plenty of rocks among which to establish territories. Unfortunately, many Rift Lake cichlids are fond of nibbling vegetation and this, coupled with their digging habits, does not encourage healthy plant growth. Plastic plants are an alternative, but anchor them into the gravel with rocks to prevent them being uprooted. Keep the water in a Rift Lake cichlid tank at about 78°F and make sure it is well aerated, hard and alkaline. Carry out regular water changes of 25 percent to keep the water free of any waste build-up. Most of these fish like to graze on algae on the rocks in the tank; good lighting encourages algal growth.

Because of their aggressive behavior, it is best to keep these cichlids only with other Rift Lake species and certain *Synodontis* catfishes as scavengers. To reduce aggression, try crowding the fish together, so that a particularly aggressive fish has plenty of rivals to pick on. If you buy all the fish at the same time, this will stop one fish establishing a territory before the others have had a chance to settle in. Many Lake Malawi cichlids are similar in appearance, which can lead to aggression when 'like' fish are kept together in the aquarium.

Lake Tanganyika cichlids are more varied in behavior, body shape and breeding technique than those from Lake Malawi. Some are mouthbrooders, while others place their eggs on rocks and guard them even after they are free-swimming. Apart from these differences they require similar care and maintenance.

Breeding Lake Malawi cichlids

These cichlids are mouthbrooders and usually quite easy to breed. The female lays eggs on the gravel or a rock, while the male swims with her in a tight circle. She then turns around to pick up the eggs with her mouth. 'Egg spot' markings on the anal fin of the male look like eggs to the female and she tries to collect them in her mouth. In doing so, she collects a mouthful of sperm instead and this fertilizes the eggs. The female keeps the eggs in her mouth until they become free-swimming fry, which can take 21-50 days. During this time, the female does not usually feed and it is advisable to remove her (with the fry) to a separate maternity tank to develop in peace. Once the fry are released from the female's mouth, they are fully developed, like little replicas of their mother.

Left: Females of the auratus cichlid (Melanochromis auratus) *from Lake Malawi have rows of black, white and yellow stripes, whereas the base color is blue in the male. These fish are rarely more than 4in long and females remain even smaller. They eat all the usual foods and thrive when kept with other Malawi cichlids in hard, alkaline water at 77°F with a pH level of 7.8-8. Do not try and keep more than one species of* Melanochromis *in the same tank, as aggression between these fish is higher than in Malawi cichlids generally. The mouthbrooding females retain their young for three to four weeks.*

Right: The zebras (Pseudotropheus zebra) *from Lake Malawi's rocky shores come in a variety of colors, depending on where they are found within the lake. Their many stripes are often absent or, at best, only partially present, and in certain color forms the male and female may have different colors. They grow to 5-6in. Males are generally more aggressive. All enjoy the usual live, freeze-dried and flake foods.*

Neotropical cichlids

From devils to angels neatly describes the neotropicals, i.e. fish from the new tropics, or American tropical areas. Included in this group are fish that range in behavior from pacifist to antagonistic; in fact, the names angels and devils are particularly appropriate. These cichlids require a large aquarium and plenty of food. They make a lot of mess and need large, regular water changes. Their real attraction is that many of them have an intelligence lacking in nearly all other fish - and most other animals for that matter. These fish will move gravel and rocks with a purpose - usually to stake out a

Below: The angelfish (Pterophyllum scalare) is silver-bronze with several black vertical bars running down through the body, although these do not always show up and the fish can change *its body colors to suit its mood or to blend in with the environment. The peaceful angelfish is the easiest of cichlids to care for and makes a good introduction to cichlid-keeping.*

Above: Through constant breeding in the aquarium trade, angelfishes rank among the hardier fishes. Color varieties and fin developments have also evolved. Gold, marble (black mottled), black (shown here) and any mixture of these are often available, as well as fish with very exaggerated fin development.

Below: This marbled angelfish, like the other varieties, is ideal for the average community. It is not overly aggressive, but make sure it does not eat smaller fish. It will live at the same temperature as most other tropicals, but prefers the water to be kept at about 79°F. It eats flake, freeze-dried and live foods.

territory and entice a mate. They recognize their owner, rushing to the tank glass for food whenever he or she approaches, and often shun strangers. Some can be taught to perform simple tricks with the inducement of an extra meal, something these greedy beasts always appreciate. When these cichlids breed, they care for the free-swimming young for quite some time, defending the minute babies from all potential predators, often regardless of the predator's size. Unfortunately, most of the larger neotropical cichlids are much bigger and more aggressive than, say, the gentle angelfish. These brutes can fight and remove scales from each other with ease, and yet they are very popular in the home aquarium and, indeed, very easy to keep, provided their requirements are met. Firstly, they need an appropriately large tank measuring at least 36in long, and even a tank this size will not house many specimens. Within this space they can exercise their normal territorial behavior; these fish become very possessive over their particular patch and will guard it fiercely from all rivals. Large cichlids eat a great deal of food and often make quite a mess with it. Large, regular water changes are therefore essential and a good mechanical filter to assist the biological filter is a help. Lastly, it is a good idea to stock fish of varying sizes and color patterns if you want them to live together in relative peace, as these fish tend to be most aggressive towards lookalikes.

Above: Jaguar cichlids (Cichlasoma managuense) from Central America are spectacular but highly aggressive. Given the right care, young specimens measuring 3-4in will grow to over 12in during their first year. Provide a 72in tank with good filtration and slightly hard water at 78°F. Feed this hungry fish with beef heart, pellets, earthworms, small fish, raw fish and other meats.

Right: The oscar (Astronotus ocellatus) can grow to 12in or more in a really large tank. The body is a mottled gray, black, olive or beige, varying according to mood, and the mucus coating gives the fish a matt appearance; these characteristics account for its other common names 'velvet', 'peacock' or 'marble' cichlid. The red oscar, the long-finned oscar and the albino oscar are all aquarium-bred lines. Oscars prefer clean water kept at about 77°F. These messy and highly aggressive fishes need a large aquarium. A 36-48in tank will suffice for a single oscar kept on its own, but if oscars are housed in pairs or with other cichlids, they need at least a 60in tank. Oscars eat almost anything: beef heart, raw fish, whitebait, earthworms, snails, cat food (dried or canned) and pellets. Once a pair have laid their eggs they guard them fiercely until they hatch.

Left: *The red devil (Cichlasoma labiatum) is a really aggressive fish, particularly towards females, and is therefore not spawned very often. Small specimens are often harmless-looking little pink creatures, but once home and established they will guard their part of the tank - which may be 100 percent of it - with ferocious vigor. The red devil is usually one color all over, anything from almost white to rich blood-red. The body is very thick and stocky with a solid head, on top of which, especially in males, you often see a nuchal hump - a large deposit of fat that develops in many cichlids with age, but particularly in this fish. This lump will also swell on the male with the advent of any sexual activity or during dominant display activity. Certain forms of the red devil develop large rubbery curled back lips. The red devil will eat a range of foods, including meat, chicken, fish, pellets and frozen foods. It does best at about 78°F and needs frequent partial water changes. The best option is to keep it alone in a pet tank. Single specimens can be kept in a 36in tank, but if the fish is to reach its potential size of 15in, it will need a tank of 60in or more. If red devils are kept together, a 72in tank is really the only viable option.*

Right: *The convicts (Cichlasoma nigrofasciatum) are some of the slightly smaller neotropical cichlids, growing to a maximum of about 7in, slightly less for females. However, they can be quite aggressive. They stem from Central America and may vary slightly in color and shape depending on their particular origin. The body color is a light gray with many vertical black bars, which makes them look just like little convicts. These fish can be rather aggressive. Any aquarium measuring 30in or more will suit them and they thrive at a temperature of 75-79°F. They greedily accept all foods. Males tend to have longer pointed dorsal and anal fins and grow larger, whereas females usually (but not always) have quite a few bright orange scales on the belly and sides. Once you have a pair of these fish in a tank they are sure to breed. They spawn on a large flat stone and the eggs hatch after only 48 hours. The young live on a large yolk sac on their belly for the first few days and can be fed on newly hatched brineshrimps as soon as they are free-swimming, usually four to five days after hatching.*

Below: Severum convictfish, or banded cichlids, (Heros severus) are very deep and quite flattened vertically. Several dark bars run down the green body and in some species there may be a scattering of wine-red spots, specially in males. They have a large red or yellow eye and a very short base to the tail. However, it is the severe look on the fish's face that accounts for its common name. This is one of the more placid species of large neotropical cichlids. It tends to prefer soft water, although it will do just as well in hard water, and relatively high temperatures of about 79°F or slightly higher. Male severums reach about 8in in the aquarium, females slightly less. These fish can be kept with other non-aggressive cichlids and non-cichlid species, provided the tank is over 36in in length. The specimen below is a very young fish.

Above: The Jack Dempsey cichlid (Cichlasoma octofasciatum) takes its common name from the legendary American heavyweight boxer, but in fact it is not as aggressive as some other cichlids. The body is quite long and slim, although it becomes bulkier with age. The eyes and mouth are rather small for a cichlid of this size. The body has eight vertical dark bars (hence the species name octofasciatum), but these do not often show up, as the whole body is covered in a profusion of metallic blue, green and gold scales that intensify in color with age. Jack Dempseys will reach about 8in or perhaps more in a really large tank, but 6in is more normal. As in most neotropical cichlids, males have longer, more pointed dorsal and anal fins, whereas females usually remain smaller than their male counterparts. These cichlids will eat a wide range of foods,

with blended beef heart being a good staple food. Other ideal foods are earthworms, pellets, and any of the frozen foods with some substance to them, such as cockle or river shrimp. It is not difficult to persuade these fish to spawn. Raising the temperature slightly from the normal 77°F to about 79°F triggers spawning, but these fish are so accommodating that often the temperature need not be altered. The pair lay and fertilize several hundred little gray eggs, usually on a rock but sometimes on the gravel. The eggs are tended by both fish and hatch after two to three days. The young live on their yolk sacs for a few days and, once free-swimming, can feed on newly hatched brineshrimp. The parents continue to care for the young until they are 0.5in long or more, but at this point the male may start to bully the female with the intention of spawning again.

Left: *The firemouth (Thorichthys meeki) has a very low, pointed snout with which it roots through the gravel for food. Its most attractive feature is the stunning red throat, especially of the male. It is one of the less aggressive cichlids; to frighten a competitor, it will blow out its gills, but this is nearly all bluff. These fish can be kept in quite small tanks of 30in or so, as they only grow to a maximum of about 6in. Firemouths eat all the usual cichlid foods and do best at temperatures of 75°F or slightly higher, in water that is slightly hard and alkaline.*

Below: *From a drab little silver fish, the quetzal cichlid (Cichlasoma synspilum) from Central America grows into a 12in-long animal, with every color of the rainbow in its scales. The head remains pink or red, and males, in particular, develop a huge head hump. Considering their size, they do not become too aggressive and can be mixed with other cichlids of a different size and coloration. Quetzals like a large aquarium, say 60in, and clean water at about 77°F. They need plenty of vegetable matter; garden peas, spinach and broad beans are good foods.*

Discus fish

Discus are universally recognized as the most beautiful and most graceful of all the freshwater aquarium fishes. They come from the warm, soft waters of South America, particularly the Amazonian rainforests. These waters are very clean and brown in color, due to staining from decaying vegetation. Discus are often found in lakes, as well as dark, slow-moving rivers.

Discus used to be regarded as very difficult to keep, and spawning them was next to impossible. Although they are still not really a beginner's fish, the availability of better equipment and increased knowledge of their needs has made the challenge somewhat easier. In the aquarium, discus fishes require a temperature of 80°F at all times and very soft, acidic water with a pH level of about 6. These very timid fish need places to hide and plants provide them with some security. However, as the fish prefer low light levels, vegetation may not grow too well, so you could use plastic plants instead. Another way of reassuring discus fishes is to introduce dither fish, such as tetras or other small characins. Dither fish are small fish that swim in the open. These give the discus the impression that the coast is clear and all is safe, so the discus are encouraged to swim out in the open, rather than hide. Discus also do better if kept in a small shoal, which makes them feel more secure. The discus tank should have a capacity of at least 24 gallons and be as deep as possible, as these fish are taller than they are long. Although they are seldom regarded as community fish, discus do well with many of the smaller non-boisterous fishes and small catfishes, but do take care that the discus' tankmates can tolerate the high water temperature and are not too small, otherwise they may be eaten. Remember, discus fishes are cichlids, after all.

Discus fish will eat all manner of food once they have become accustomed to it, but it must be small enough to fit into their tiny mouths. They enjoy finely blended beef heart, bloodworm, *Daphnia* and flake food, as well as freeze-dried *Tubifex*. Never feed live *Tubifex* worms to discus as they contain so much bacterial matter that they are potentially fatal. Discus need very clean water, so carry out frequent and methodical water changes, and clean the gravel with a gravel washer.

Left: The brown discus shown here (Symphysodon aequifasciatus) *is the more common of the two species of discus fish. There are two subspecies of the brown discus, one blue, one green. The body is extremely compressed vertically and when viewed head-on appears very narrow. Several bright blue lines cross the body; in the brown discus they may only occur on the face.*

Breeding discus fish

There are no real differences between male and female discus fish, so to obtain a pair, buy half a dozen fish and let them pair off. Discus spawn in the typical cichlid method, females laying eggs on a rock or leaf to be fertilized by the male. Discus fish always choose a vertical spawning site, often favoring the uplift of the undergravel filter. The female fans and guards the eggs while the male guards the immediate territory. After three days, the eggs hatch and the adults move the young to another site, where they are stuck by little sticky filaments. The young live on a yolk sac for a few days and eventually become free-swimming. At this stage, an amazing phenomenon takes place. The young rise up and start to feed from the skin of the adult fish, each of the adults taking their turn to feed the young. After about 10 days, the young need other food to supplement the mucus from the parents' skin, so offer them newly hatched brineshrimp.

Left: Symphysodon aequifasciata haraldi. *All the discus fish have large eyes that range in color from orange to bright red. Usually, these fish are not sold at less than 2in in diameter. However, with good care they can reach up to 6in across and at this size command a high price and look really stunning. Whatever the species, all discus fish require the same care.*

Anabantids

Anabantids are a very popular group of fishes from Asia and Africa, most of which are known as gouramis. These fish have a special extra breathing organ called the 'labyrinth', which is a bunch of folded tissues with many blood vessels within it. This organ enables the fishes to extract the oxygen from air taken in at the surface, which is very useful in water with low oxygen levels. However, gouramis have evolved to depend so much on this organ that now they cannot exist without regularly taking air from the surface, regardless of the water's oxygen content. The air is also used to construct what are usually described as 'bubblenests'. The male fishes build these nests on the surface of the water with air and their saliva and attach them to any floating debris. Most anabantids are undemanding and relatively peaceful compared to other fishes, although often they do not get along too well with their own kind.

Below: The pearl, leeri or mosaic gourami (Trichogaster leeri) *grows to about 4in. The long, compressed body is blue-brown with a smothering of pearl spots. Maintain the aquarium water at 78°F and carry out regular water changes. This fish accepts all foods, but relishes live food. It spawns in a bubblenest; raise the fry on liquid fry food or newly hatched brineshrimp.*

Above: The lovely dwarf gourami (Colisa lalia) *only grows to about 2.5in in total length and is completely peaceful - a superb aquarium subject. Males are much more colorful than females. Water conditions are not critical, but maintain the temperature at about 78°F and avoid acidic water. Dwarf gouramis often live in one of the top corners of the tank and prefer a little shade, so if their tank is brightly lit, provide some floating plants, such as duckweed, for cover. They relish live foods and will also accept flake, dried and frozen foods. When they spawn, the male builds a bubblenest and then entices the female to it. After spawning, remove the female to avoid the risk of bullying. The fry can be difficult to raise and may require food as small as infusoria, rather than liquid fry food.*

Left: In the three-spot, or blue, gourami (Trichogaster trichopterus) the body is light blue with several darker vertical patches. There is a black spot in the middle of the body and at the base of the tail, and the eye makes up the third spot. There are several color variants of this species, including light blue specimens with no spots (above) or even gold specimens (below). Take care when keeping this species in pairs, as males can be very aggressive towards females and if there is no escape, the female may be bullied to death. Keep the water clean, provide some plants for cover and also some open space for the fish to swim around in. This gourami readily accepts all foods, but prefers live food.

Above: *Paradisefish* (Macropodus opercularis) *are often available, but unfortunately, males can be rather aggressive, especially towards one another during the breeding season, so they do not mix very well. Females are slightly smaller and less colorful than males. This very hardy little Asian fish can survive in water with temperatures as low as 55°F, although at these temperatures it is nowhere near as colorful. Water composition is not important, but the fish appreciate some plant cover and subdued lighting. They greedily accept all foods, particularly small live foods. Paradisefish breed at the warmer temperature of 75°F in typical anabantid fashion; take care that the female is not fatally bullied.*

Right: *The giant gourami* (Osphronemus gourami) *grows 24in long and is best kept as a single specimen 'pet' in a very large tank or with other large species. The whole body is covered in large light to dark gray scales which, although not colorful, create an interesting pattern. This fish is very happy in hard water at about 75°F. It is vital to keep the water clean, which may be a problem as they eat a great deal of food and create so much waste. Good biological filtration is essential; for best results, couple this with an external mechanical filter. Giant gouramis eat everything from canned or garden peas, baked beans, spinach, lettuce, grapes and cooked apple to worms, beef heart and raw fish.*

Siamese fighting fish

The infamous Siamese fighting fish *(Betta splendens)* can only be second to the piranha for tales of terror and yet this fish is only aggressive towards its own kind. Siamese fighting fish come from Thailand (formerly known as Siam), where they live in small pools and ditches. Each male *Betta* has its own small territory, where it builds and repairs its little bubblenest, defending it avidly from any other male *Betta*. If two males come together, they fight so viciously that if neither retreats then at least one will die. Male fighters are easy to keep in a tank, but clearly you should never keep two males together. It is also unwise to keep females with males unless the intention is to breed them. Males are often overly aggressive to females that do not wish to spawn.

To breed Siamese fighting fish, set up a tank with a low water level, say about 6in, and no filtration to cause movement at the water surface. Add some hiding places for the female and a tightly fitting lid to trap a layer of warm air. Place the male and female in the tank with a divider between them and feed them heavily with live food. Raise the temperature to 83°F. The male will build a nest of bubbles in one of the top corners and then go in search of the female. At this point, carefully lift the divider and, if all goes well, the female will be enticed under the nest, where the fish embrace, with the male wrapped around the female. She then expels her eggs and the male fertilizes them. As they fall to the bottom, the male catches them in his mouth and places them within the bubblenest. The female lies motionlessly on her side under the nest, and the sequence is repeated until all the eggs are laid. Remove the female at this stage. The male tends the nest and the fry hatch out after about two days. Remove the male three days later. The free-swimming fry need microscopic live food, such as infusoria, to begin with, graduating to newly hatched brineshrimp. After another week, the labyrinth gland starts to develop and there may be many losses at this point. After a further two weeks, the males start bickering, so separate them into their own little jars This is quite safe, as they need little room to move around and can breathe from the surface.

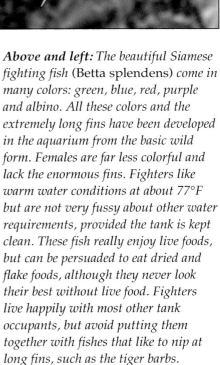

Above and left: The beautiful Siamese fighting fish (Betta splendens) *come in many colors: green, blue, red, purple and albino. All these colors and the extremely long fins have been developed in the aquarium from the basic wild form. Females are far less colorful and lack the enormous fins. Fighters like warm water conditions at about 77°F but are not very fussy about other water requirements, provided the tank is kept clean. These fish really enjoy live foods, but can be persuaded to eat dried and flake foods, although they never look their best without live food. Fighters live happily with most other tank occupants, but avoid putting them together with fishes that like to nip at long fins, such as the tiger barbs.*

Zebra lionfish (Dendrochirus zebra)

CREATING YOUR OWN MARINE AQUARIUM

The earth's tropical oceans are the planet's most stable environment. A relatively short distance below the surface, and away from the shoreline, nothing changes from day to night, from winter to summer or from year to year. The parameters of the fishes' surroundings are incredibly constant - the temperature, the salinity, the pH level, the oxygen content, the very composition of the water is never-changing. It follows, therefore, that a typical marine fish has no built-in mechanism for change and it is this that makes the hobby of keeping marine fishes such a challenge. If the aquarist does not take care to create a similarly unchanging environment for his charges, then disaster looms. Unlike their freshwater counterparts, marine fishes do not adapt readily to life in an aquarium and rarely breed in captivity. As a result, the vast majority of all captive marine fishes are wild-caught and must be treated with greater respect than even the most temperamental freshwater fishes.

All this may make the prospect of keeping marine fishes sound rather daunting, but when housed in the right conditions, there is no reason why they should not thrive. This part of the book builds on the foundations laid down in the practical pages of the freshwater section. Many of the same basic principles apply to setting up and maintaining a marine aquarium, but the important exceptions are carefully described and explained. With the wide range of specialist equipment available today, keeping marines is well within the scope of the enthusiastic and dedicated fishkeeper.

Setting up a marine aquarium

The step-by-step photographs featured on pages 84-89

The type of tank you choose will depend on the location you have in mind, how you want it to look, and the amount of money you have to spend. As for freshwater tropical fishes, virtually every marine tank is made from glass panels sealed with aquarium sealant, although there are models that incorporate plastic or wood-grain trimming to improve their final appearance. It is important to avoid metal trims and appendages because these will quickly corrode when exposed to salt water. The tank should have a tight-fitting sliding cover glass, which not only prevents fish escaping, but also reduces evaporation (which upsets the salt balance), prevents water splashing out, and keeps out unwelcome intruders, whether they be cats, children, or simply dust, fumes and aerosol sprays.

As far as size is concerned, there is no absolute minimum size aquarium in which to keep marine fishes, but it is advisable to consider a tank holding about 28 gallons as the least allowable, and one holding 42 gallons or more as preferable. Transferred into sizes, this means that you should start off with a tank measuring no less than 36x12x15in in length, width and depth, although one measuring 36x15x18in would be better. The actual dimensions are irrelevant, however, because it is the finished volume of water that is the sole criterion for size considerations.

Marine aquariums can be divided into two sorts: simple boxes, with or without adornment and hood arrangements; and complete systems, with all or much of the equipment included within the fabric of the tank. The step-by-step photographs featured on pages 84-89 show how to set up a small and very basic all-glass marine aquarium. In many ways, the sequence follows the same basic steps involved in setting up the freshwater aquarium as described on pages 12-19. The major differences are that the water will be salty and that the 'life-support' systems, such as lighting, heating and filtration, need to function more efficiently and within stricter tolerances to support the more sensitive marine creatures displayed in the finished aquarium. The captions to the setting up photographs reflect the practical steps involved, while the main text discusses more general points concerned with filtration, lighting, heating, salt balance and testing equipment.

Filtration systems for the marine aquarium

If you were to set up an aquarium without fish, then there would be no need to filter the water. However, as soon as you add animals and food, the resulting waste products pollute the water. The ideal filtration system is for a constant flow of water to pass through the

Below: Place an undergravel filter plate in the base of the tank, just as you would for a freshwater system. Before you do this, make sure that you place a slab of styrofoam about 0.5in thick beneath the tank to support it and to cushion any irregularities in the surface of the stand. If you have any doubts about the tank, test it outdoors by filling it with water and checking it for leaks.

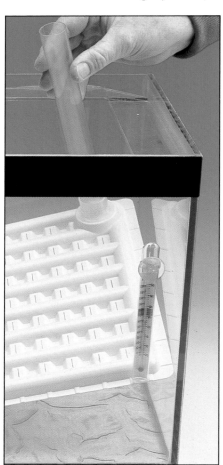

Above: Cover the entire surface of the filter plate with a layer of well-washed coarse medium, such as coral gravel or dolomite chippings. You can buy this from your aquarium dealer. Do not use the kind of gravel recommended for freshwater systems. Spread the medium out into a layer about 2in deep.

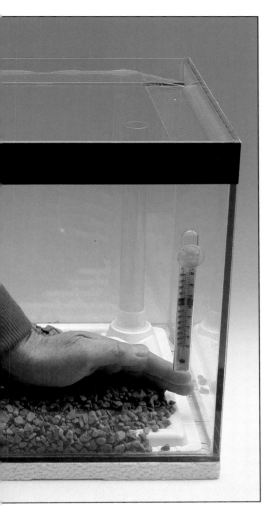

aquarium, with new clean water replacing the old polluted water. This is not exactly practical unless you live next to a tropical shoreline, where it is used by the occasional public aquarium.

However, back in the real world of modest-sized tanks in the living room, it is necessary to devise small practical filtration units for home use. Although we have reviewed the basic operation of filtration systems for freshwater tanks on page 14, the subject bears repeating here because of the more precise control over water quality demanded by marine fishes.

Filtration can be divided into three types - physical, biological and chemical. As the name suggests, physical filtration simply involves physically removing waste matter. This is the ideal method, but it usually only works with large granular matter, and would not work with, for instance, liquid waste. Biological filtration involves bacteria beds that 'biologically' consume waste matter, and this method of filtration is the basis of successful marine keeping. Chemical filtration involves chemically removing or absorbing waste matter, usually by means of an agent, such as activated carbon. An ideal marine system usually makes use of these three methods of filtration in combination.

Most marine systems are set up around an undergravel filter bed, the mechanics of which provide the necessary biological filtration. The complete system ideally consists of an undergravel filter plate that fits the entire base of the tank, covered by a 2in layer of coarse aggregate, such as coral gravel or dolomite chippings, covered by a further layer of coral sand, the two media being separated by a plastic mesh (called a 'gravel tidy') to prevent intermixing. Water is then drawn down through the media and up the uplift tube, either by means of an external air pump creating a rising column of bubbles, or more efficiently, by means of a water pump (a so-called 'power head') situated on top of the uplift tube. The nitrifying bacteria that flourish in the gravel and sand layers 'consume' the fishes' waste products and convert them to less harmful substances. In simple terms, nitrifying bacteria have a few basic needs in order to flourish - a surface on which to cling (the gravel/sand particles),

Above: Trim a gravel tidy (a sheet of plastic mesh) to fit the tank and place it, curl downwards, over the medium. This will prevent mixing of the media and prevent fish digging down to the plate.

Below: Then add a 2in layer of unwashed coral sand on top of the gravel tidy mesh. You can see the two layers clearly in this photograph. Slope this layer down to the front of the tank.

Undergravel filtration using a power head

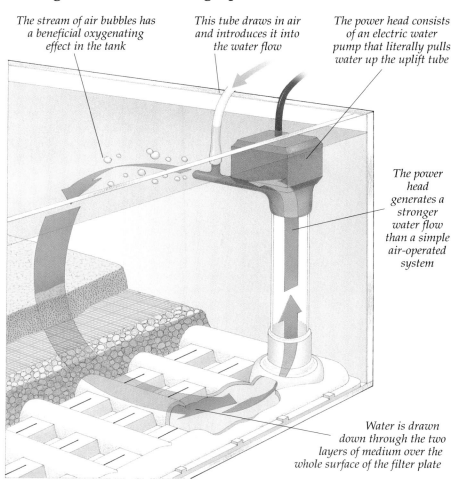

The stream of air bubbles has a beneficial oxygenating effect in the tank

This tube draws in air and introduces it into the water flow

The power head consists of an electric water pump that literally pulls water up the uplift tube

The power head generates a stronger water flow than a simple air-operated system

Water is drawn down through the two layers of medium over the whole surface of the filter plate

Above: Using a power head at the top of the uplift tube creates a strong and consistent flow of water through the undergravel filtration system. It is vital to maintain good water conditions in the marine aquarium and such an arrangement helps to keep the biological filter bed working at top efficiency. Compare the water flow here with the reverse flow system shown on page 87.

plenty of oxygen (drawn from the well-oxygenated water flow), and a food supply (the nitrogenous waste products).

An efficient undergravel filter not only provides biological filtration, but also acts as a physical filter, as solid debris is drawn into and trapped by the coral sand. This can be a disadvantage, as the coral sand can get dirty and clogged. Although it is possible to add an outside canister filter in order to try and remove debris from the water flow before it clogs the sand, an alternative arrangement is to set up a reverse-flow biological system. To do this, direct the water flow from the outlet pipe of a canister filter (containing physical and chemical filter media) into the uplift tube of the undergravel filter. In this way, cleaned water from the outside canister filter is forced underneath the undergravel filter plate and up through the layers of gravel and sand. This method is far more efficient than the standard flow biological system, and can be recommended to beginners and more experienced aquarists alike.

It is worth mentioning trickle filtration here. An undergravel filter is quite 'wasteful' of resources, since nitrifying bacteria are naturally 'dry' creatures, and when they are submerged, they drown and have to mutate constantly in order to survive and propagate. Trickle filter systems have the filter medium in small containers above the water and a trickle of water is passed over them. This system is far more effective in the sense that one small container of porous gravel can hold as many nitrifying bacteria as a large submerged filter bed, but its disadvantage is that only so much water can be passed over it before it becomes submerged.

There are several manufactured systems that incorporate trickle filter units, whether as separate components that you attach to your tank or as part of a complete built-in aquarium management

Right: This is a simple air-powered protein skimmer. The rising stream of bubbles creates a froth in the upper part of the skimmer and molecules of organic waste in the water cling onto the surface of the bubbles and are carried over the lip into a collecting cup at the top. The froth collapses into a yellowish liquid, which can be emptied from the cup. More sophisticated models set up a countercurrent flow of water and air so the bubbles stay in contact with the water for a longer period. There are also versions fitted with an electric pump.

Below: With the undergravel filter plate and the gravel and sand in place, you can add the heater/thermostat and connect up the power head and air pump. Note the air diffuser at left.

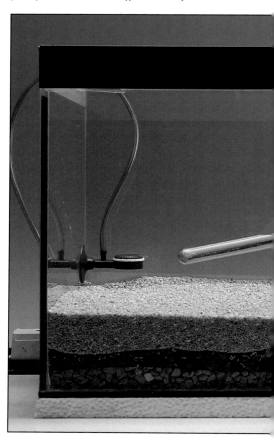

system. Some aquarium set-ups combine both trickle filters and undergravel filters. In fact, once you understand the fundamental principles involved, there is no reason why you should not build your own filtration system using both these methods.

The third part of the filtration jigsaw is chemical filtration. In order to supplement biological and physical filtration, many aquarists use activated carbon and other proprietary filter media, usually placed in a box or canister filter, which absorb waste products. Carbon is particularly useful in absorbing phenols, which would otherwise tint the water yellow, but has the disadvantage of not being obvious when its useful life is over. Some proprietary filter media not only have much greater absorption capabilities than carbon, but also indicate when they are spent by changing color.

One disadvantage of absorbent materials, however, is that they also absorb copper compounds, which are a major ingredient in disease treatments, at least in a fish-only aquarium. An alternative method of chemical filtration is a piece of equipment called a protein skimmer, a slightly cumbersome unit that 'strips' the sea water of excess protein. Modern aquarists regard this as an essential addition to a system, its presence giving a stability previously unknown, but it is not always easy to find room for one, particularly since the top collecting cup has to sit just above the water level. For smaller tanks, inexpensive air-driven models are fine, but for larger tanks a more expensive motor driven unit is advisable.

Finally on filtration, we should mention two further items of filtration: ozonizers and ultraviolet sterilizers, both comparatively expensive. Although either or both of these pieces of equipment are beneficial, we advise any potential aquarists that they could spend their money more usefully at this stage, and at least for the time being they should not worry themselves over these expensive acquisitions.

Reverse-flow undergravel filtration

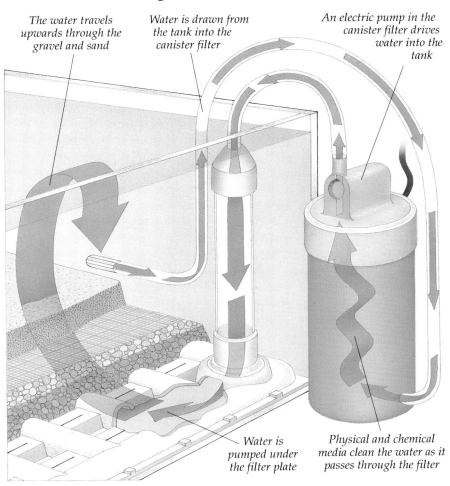

The water travels upwards through the gravel and sand

Water is drawn from the tank into the canister filter

An electric pump in the canister filter drives water into the tank

Water is pumped under the filter plate

Physical and chemical media clean the water as it passes through the filter

Above: This is how an outside canister filter - often called a power filter - can be used to pre-clean the water before it flows through the undergravel filtration system in the reverse direction, i.e. upwards rather than downwards. This arrangement helps to keep the coral gravel and sand clear of clogging detritus so that it can fulfil its biological cleaning role more efficiently.

What do 'specific gravity' and 'salinity' mean?

Both terms reflect the saltiness of water. Basically, the more salt in the water - and here the word 'salt' refers to a mix of salts, in which sodium chloride dominates - the higher is its specific gravity and salinity. The two measurements are quite distinct, however, and are expressed in different units.

Specific gravity

This is the ratio of the density of a liquid compared to the density of distilled water, which is said to have a specific gravity of 1. In the marine aquarium, 'healthy' values hover around 1.020, and very small changes in specific gravity represent significant variations in salt concentration for the marine creatures.

Salinity

This is a measure of the salt concentration in water, and is expressed in grams/liter (parts per thousand). There is a close relationship between salinity and specific gravity, but it alters with temperature. At 75°F, for example, a specific gravity of 1.020 is equivalent to a salinity of 29.8 gm/liter. As the temperature rises, the salinity required to maintain a specific gravity of 1.020 also rises. This is why it so important to measure and stabilize the specific gravity of the water in your aquarium at the final operating temperature.

Lighting a marine tank

Lighting plays an important part in the marine aquarium, for the simple reason that the world's coral reefs are all subject to strong sunlight all the year round, and many of the reef's inhabitants need that sunlight to survive. Also, many of the more colorful show fish, angels and tangs in particular, need algae as an essential part of their diet, and the only way to grow algae is to have sufficient light in the aquarium. Therefore, your tank should incorporate quite strong artificial lighting. There are a number of ways to achieve this. Most simple tanks are supplied with a metal or plastic hood designed to hold a number of fluorescent tubes. Do make sure that the hood is easily removable for easy access, and remember to ensure that the cover glasses are watertight. If the hood is metal, coat it with three layers of polyurethane varnish to ward off corrosion.

There is a huge variety of fluorescent tubes available, many of them especially formulated for the aquarium fish market. This form of lighting is ideal because fluorescent tubes are not too expensive to buy, are economical to run, last a long time and do not run hot. They are sufficient for most marine tanks, but you may need something more penetrative for deeper tanks, and for situations where lush growths of algae are required. Do remember that fluorescent tubes only have a limited useful life, even if they continue to give off light. Replace the lights in rotation so that there are always one or two tubes that are less than six months old.

Because of the bulkiness of marine lighting arrangements, many aquarists choose tanks without hoods. You can then either situate the tank in the open and use decorative lighting, or you can enclose the tank behind a wall or partition and make use of standard, perhaps unattractive, but also less expensive lighting simply suspended over the tank. Ordinary domestic spotlights can be positioned over an aquarium, with the light directed into the water to create some striking effects in moving water.

Mercury vapor lamps are increasingly popular lighting for aquariums. These look like decorative household lights, and are either suspended over the aquarium or are wall mounted. They are quite expensive but they are a very efficient light source, and can be recommended in those situations where they can be fitted.

Metal halide lamps would be the specialists' choice. Anybody who has seen a large marine tank lit by metal halide lamps would be hard put to go back to 'ordinary' lighting without feeling dissatisfied. These lighting units, suitably protected for use near the aquarium, are expensive and bulky, however, and may not be suitable for beginners to marine fishkeeping. One final word on lighting and tank location. Although it is not a good idea to locate a freshwater tank in direct sunlight, marine tanks can prosper in sunlight, and a warm conservatory or similar situation makes an ideal location.

Above: With the main decorations in place, add the required amount of dry salt mix according to the panel opposite.

Above: Add warm water slowly so as not to disturb the existing decor and allow a margin for adding further items.

Above: Fitting a cover glass or plastic condensation tray prevents any fishes jumping out and cuts evaporation of water to a minimum. On larger tanks you can fit more than one cover glass.

How much salt to add?

Multiply the tank length, width and depth in inches and divide the result by 230 to obtain the volume in gallons. If you are adding solid decorations, reduce this by 20% for displacement by multiplying the volume by 0.8. Then multiply the number of gallons by 2.8 and this will be the weight of salt needed in pounds. (If the pack instructions are geared toward liters and kilograms, multiply the number of gallons by 3.8 to convert to liters and follow the directions.) Check the specific gravity using a hydrometer when the aquarium is up and running and add water or salt as necessary.

Below: This is a swing-needle type of hydrometer that clearly shows the specific gravity of your aquarium water. Simply place this device in the tank, but make sure that you test the water at its recommended operating temperature. Ideally, aim for a reading of 1.020.

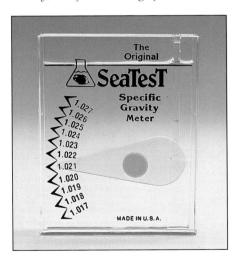

Heating a marine aquarium

Marine aquarium systems need to be kept at the same temperature as freshwater ones, i.e. 75°F. But marine fish are far more intolerant of temperature fluctuations than freshwater fish, and so it is important to buy reliable heating equipment. For a centrally heated 'average' home environment buy a heater/thermostat with a rating that allows 10 watts for every gallon of water in the aquarium. In a colder environment, increase this allowance to 12 watts. Since even the best heater will fail eventually, and invariably when the local shop is closed, buy two half-size heaters for all except the smallest tanks, rather than buying one main heater and one spare. Then, if one heater fails, the other will cope until you replace it or, if one heater sticks in the on position, it will take far longer to raise the temperature to dangerous levels, and give you far more advanced warning.

A word here about thermometers. Glass thermometers are available filled with spirit or mercury. Both sorts are inconvenient to read, and mercury ones are lethal if they break, while spirit models are usually unreliable. The stick-on digital thermometers are the best to choose for marine tanks as they are for freshwater ones. Although their reading is not too accurate, they will record temperature fluctuations fairly accurately. But it is a good idea to check their accuracy with a mercury thermometer briefly suspended in the tank.

Synthetic sea water

It may be difficult to understand why natural sea water is inferior to artificial sea water. After all, it is obviously good enough for the fish that live in it. Let us assume that you live near the coast, and collecting sea water would not be expensive or inconvenient - big assumptions! Firstly, natural sea water is usually polluted, especially near the shore, so it would be necessary to collect it offshore. Secondly, natural sea water is full of 'life', including plankton, much of which would die in a home environment, thus creating a pollution problem. It is also likely that a great deal of the life forms would be disease organisms, which would attack your tank's future inhabitants.

Below: With the hood fitted and the lights on, the aquarium begins to look like a miniature portion of the tropical ocean. At this stage you can fit the protein skimmer, but do not start it, and run any power filters with just biological media, not chemical. Leave everything running for 24 hours or so. By the next day, the water should be clear, the temperature should have stabilized, and the specific gravity should be around 1.020. You will now need to mature the system, by adding a proprietary agent. If you have a friend with a marine tank, 'borrow' a cup of mature sand to hasten the process. The system will take between ten days and a month to mature. Measure the nitrite level regularly. At first there should be no reading, but as you add the maturation agent, the nitrite reading will steadily increase. After a week or so it will peak and remain high, and then one day it will suddenly fall to zero.

Decorating a marine aquarium

The decor you choose may be either 'dead' or 'alive.' The former refers to dead coral and shells, and various types of both natural and man-made rocks. Live decoration includes 'living rock' and various living but generally stationary invertebrates. You may wish to start with dead decor and graduate to living decor at a later stage.

Corals and shells

Dead coral and shells were once a popular method of decoration, but our awareness of the problems of habitat destruction has radically changed our thinking. Hard corals, whether dead or alive, are now listed under the CITES regulations to prevent their international export, and are therefore becoming increasingly less available. Nevertheless, pieces are still around and available for aquarists' use. Unless you are assured that the pieces have been pre-treated, then you should treat any chosen piece yourself to ensure that the coral, or in particular the shell, does not contain any of the original living inhabitant. To do this immerse the corals for 24 hours in a solution of household bleach made with one cup per gallon of water. In the case of shells, ensure that the bleach gets right into the core. After this period of soaking, put the pieces under running water for 48 hours or so, until there is not the slightest smell of chlorine in the air. Again, ensure that inner crevices are thoroughly washed before using pieces in the tank.

Arranging decorations within the tank

When you arrange the decor, remember that your fish will not be bright enough to understand which is the front of the tank and which is the rear. Therefore, although you need to give the fish some places to hide, do leave plenty of free swimming places at the front, so that the fish will choose this area as their natural gathering and exercise territory. Take time and trouble to ensure that any rocks are solidly placed so that they will not tumble if the base sand is disturbed. A surprising number of fishes and invertebrates seem to delight in rearranging your carefully placed sand. And do not lean any rocks against equipment such as heaters or filters; you will regret it when you need to change or adjust these devices. If you choose to bury an air diffuser within a piece of coral or a shell, remember to put a convenient join in the airline so that you can change the diffuser easily - they block up amazingly frequently.

Using rockwork

A sensible approach to decorating the marine tank is to use rockwork. Suitable natural rocks include tufa rock, slates, sandstones and most types of granite. Ensure that the rocks you choose are clean; often a good clean with a stiff brush is all that is required. If you feel that granites and similar rocks do not

Below: This is sheer indulgence to show such a magnificent aquarium, but it does demonstrate how wonderful a fully decorated marine tank can look. The term 'fully decorated' in this case refers not only to structural decorations but also embraces a host of invertebrate animals compatible with the fishes. This is a scene to motivate every beginner.

Artificial corals

Artificial corals made from fiberglass are an ideal substitute for the real thing. Not only are these environmentally safe, but they are also available in the natural colors of the original live coral, rather than just in bleached white. While white corals look very attractive at first, they soon become coated with algae and slime; artificial corals overcome both the moral and aesthetic objections.

look sufficiently exotic, there are a number of man-made materials that have a more realistic 'submarine' and craggy appearance. These are also far more porous, and therefore do not displace so much water as the real thing. One in particular, called grotto rock, is ideal to intermix with living rock (see below), and another, lava rock, has a red hue particularly effective under a red light. You can also buy simulated rock pieces and low walls that can be useful to hide equipment and create ledges in the aquarium.

Using 'living rock'

The ideal decoration is known as 'living rock', and is in fact pieces of coral rock hewn from the coral beds, the best pieces coming from the Red Sea. Every piece is different, often interestingly shaped and full of small holes and caves, and each contains a host of sea life, including corals, polyps, algae, crustaceans and sea urchins. These creatures may be in a planktonic form, which often develop into adult forms if the tank's other inhabitants allow them to. There is no doubt that living rock is the most natural, the most beautiful, the most useful, and the most healthy type of decoration to choose for a marine aquarium.

If you do choose living rock, then do not buy it until the tank is fully ready. However, you can use it to mature the tank naturally instead of a chemical agent. If you buy a large amount, you will find that you will get a very high and protracted nitrite reading, and you will need to perform a large water change after the tank is matured, before introducing the fish. If you use only a small amount of living rock to mature a tank, it is still better to buy at least most of the required amount before going onto mobile animals, if for no other reason than that it is unfair on sensitive marine creatures to keep disturbing them in their new environment.

Living rock has a few disadvantages, not least its high cost, which rules it out as an option for many aquarists. One way of reducing the financial strain is to lay a foundation of cheaper rockwork and then cover this with living rock, from where at least some of the life will travel and encrust the dead pieces. A second drawback of living rock is that you have no control over the types of life it contains. It is no use complaining afterwards if you discover that you have inadvertently introduced a vicious predator, such as a mantis shrimp, or unleashed a colony of bristleworms. These worms are harmless but incredibly fertile, and quite a few aquarists have ended up with a tank literally seething with a mass of unremovable worms. A third problem with living rock is that since it contains life, it is counted as an invertebrate, and thus prevents medication being used in disease prevention. With these points in mind, a fish-only aquarium is in many ways far easier and far cheaper than a more natural mixed fish/invertebrate system, especially for beginners.

Above: In somewhat more restrained surroundings, a flame angelfish (Centropyge loriculus) *wends it way over tufa rocks festooned with red algae and among the green, almost artificial-looking fronds of a seaweed called* Caulerpa. *This is surprisingly easy to raise in a brightly lit marine aquarium.*

Feeding and maintenance

Apart from propagating their line, marine fish spend their lives either finding food or ensuring that they are not part of another fish's meal. Usually there is no shortage of either choice or quantity of food available, because the coral reefs represent an almost perfect model of a well-balanced food chain.

Fish naturally divide into various types of feeders - damselfishes, clown anemonefishes and gobies, for example, are filter feeders, almost automatically passing minute particles of food into their stomachs. Tangs are grazers; butterflyfishes are pickers; angelfishes both graze and pick; triggers, lionfishes and groupers are predators; and wrasses and goatfishes are scavengers. Some fish are vegetarian - tangs in particular - whereas some are carnivorous, such as lionfishes; most are omnivorous, taking a range of foods.

Fulfilling all the marine fishes' natural dietary demands in the home aquarium is not always easy, especially bearing in mind the need to carefully monitor feeding levels and to ensure that no excess food is ever introduced into the system. Not only is it vital never to leave uneaten food in the water because of pollution, but it is also important not to allow the fish to over-indulge themselves. Ensuring that shyer fish get their fair share of food to meet their dietary requirements, while there are more aggressive fish eating everything available, is quite a skill, and one that every successful marine fishkeeper needs to develop.

Many of the fish in the home aquarium, such as damsels, clowns, wrasses, most angels, a few butterflyfishes and most tangs, will readily take either flake or granular food. These are obviously the most convenient of foodstuffs as far as the aquarist is concerned, but even if all the tank's inhabitants take them readily, it is important to vary the diet by also feeding a range of frozen foods. As well as being fresher and richer in vitamins, which are important for the fishes' well-being, such foods also offer a variety of tastes, textures and shapes that a single processed food cannot provide.

Above: A yellow tang and angelfish come to investigate some lettuce leaves weighed down with a magnetic cleaner pad. These vegetarian fishes will graze algae and also take other vegetable foods. Soften lettuce and spinach leaves by blanching briefly in boiling water.

Above: A cube boxfish takes a piece of shellfish meat directly from its owner's hand - a sign of confidence for both parties. You can buy frozen shellfish meat from your aquarium dealer and thaw out portions as required. These foods are convenient and disease-free.

Below: These are typical frozen foods that can be fed to suitable marine fishes. They are supplied in flat frozen packs that will keep for several months in the freezer. You can simply break off a piece of the food when needed, thaw it out and feed it to your fish. The foods are irradiated to kill off any aquatic pests and so they present no health risk.

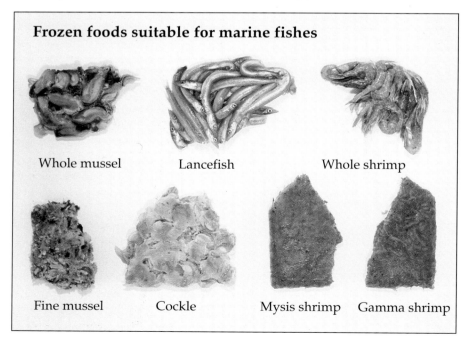

Frozen foods suitable for marine fishes

Whole mussel   Lancefish   Whole shrimp

Fine mussel   Cockle   Mysis shrimp   Gamma shrimp

Maintenance check list

❏ Check your aquarium water on a regular basis so that you can keep it in top condition.

❏ Maintain the pH value of the water in the range 8.1-8.3.

❏ Always keep the specific gravity between 1.019 and 1.021.

❏ Never allow any nitrite to appear, nor allow nitrates to exceed 30ppm (parts per million/equivalent to milligrams per liter).

❏ Make regular water changes (a minimum of the equivalent of 25 percent per month).

❏ Keep your fluorescent tubes fresh (as explained on page 88).

❏ Always have a ready supply of replacement air diffusers.

❏ Never be tempted to use unsterilized seafoods, such as prawns and mussels, including live wild shrimps.

❏ Check and replace filter media when necessary.

Frozen foods can be bought as individual types, such as *Mysis* shrimp, brineshrimp, lancefish, mussel meat, etc., or preferably as complete diets. If access to frozen food is impossible, it is important to feed a variety of different dry foods, and to add a vitamin supplement more often than if using frozen foods. Freeze-dried krill, bloodworm, and *Gammarus* shrimps can all be used as additions to flake and granules.

Regular maintenance

It is especially important to concentrate on two areas of regular maintenance - equipment and water quality. Check the equipment regularly. Replace fluorescent tubes on a regular basis to maintain light levels in the aquarium, and check and overhaul the air pumps, power heads and power filters to a predetermined maintenance schedule. Always keep a supply of spare parts, such as diaphragms, rotors and sealing rings, for these vital pieces of equipment. Check heaters for accuracy, replace airstones at the first sign of blocking, and clean or replace the filter medium as necessary.

When the aquarium is first established, we assume that the water quality is at its optimum. Certain parameters can be measured - equipment or kits are available for determining temperature, specific gravity, ammonia, nitrite, nitrate, pH and oxygen levels. There are many more components to keep track of but these are beyond the hobbyist's scope. Experience has shown, however, that if the measurable parameters are all in order then the tank's well-being is virtually assured.

The first step, therefore, is to buy and use reliable kits and testing equipment. The very minimum from the above list would be a thermometer, a hydrometer (used for determining specific gravity), plus nitrite, nitrate and pH test kits. Keep a log and take action at the slightest deterioration in standards. It is vital to maintain a testing regime so that the various readings are correct on a consistent basis; it is too late to take corrective action when the pH value of the water, for example, has strayed out of the range 8.1-8.3.

The simple, all-embracing way to maintain water quality is to institute a regular regime of partial water changes. An average of 10 percent per week is the ideal, but so many factors will have an effect on the percentage, such as size of tank, sophistication of filtering equipment, number of fish, and primarily, of course, the amount of food introduced. Before adding new water to the aquarium, premix it to the correct salinity and temperature, and then aerate it for a few hours before use. To remove the appropriate amount of water from the aquarium use a siphon tube fitted with a gravel washer attachment. Dig this through the sand to remove all sludge and detritus. As part of this regular maintenance routine keep the cover glass clean and front glass of the aquarium clear of algae.

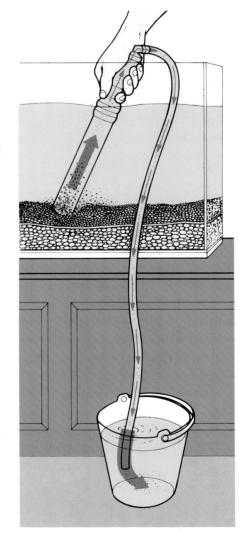

Below: You can use a gravel washer such as this one when making partial water changes. With this model you start up the siphon flow by plunging the plastic cylinder up and down in the aquarium with the opening held below the water level. As water flows out of the aquarium you can agitate the substrate with the cylinder so that debris is carried away. There is a filter at the top of the cylinder to prevent fish and substrate particles being removed.

Basic marine health care

Maintaining a healthy marine aquarium is so much easier if you take a few elementary steps to prevent diseases occurring in the first place. Always buy your fish carefully from a respected and proven shop, where the livestock is well cared for and quarantined before sale. Never buy a fish that has not been in the country for at least two weeks, try and see it feeding before you buy it, and inspect it closely before taking it home. If the fish has any marks, spots, irregularities, tears, blemishes, in fact, if it is any way less than perfect, save your money!

Once the fish has been bagged, leave it in darkness until you get it home; do not keep inspecting it to see if it is all right. Once home, switch off the tank lights and expose the fish to dim daylight. Place the whole sealed plastic bag into the aquarium water and leave it there for 30 minutes, in order for the two water temperatures to equalize. Then tip the water and fish into a clean, clear, plastic container that can float in the top of the aquarium. For the next 60 minutes gradually add aquarium water to the plastic container. Finally, net the fish into the aquarium and discard all the water in the container. Leave the tank lights off until the following day.

However carefully you try to stick to any guidelines to reduce stress and prevent disease organisms entering the aquarium, sooner or later, a disease will appear. Since all marine fish are so intolerant of changing surroundings, and since every marine fish should be regarded as a swimming time bomb full of potential disease, eventually disease will break out. In simplest terms, diseases can be divided into two categories - a few readily recognizable, treatable diseases, and all the rest. Fortunately, it is the recognizable and treatable diseases that are often highly contagious, whereas most other diseases are often limited to the original host fish.

The recognizable diseases include marine white spot, coral fish disease and flukes. All of them are characterized by spots of different sizes and colors on the fish, and all can be treated, fairly simply, by adding proprietary medications based on copper sulfate to the tank water. Almost without exception, these medications work

A marine medicine chest

The following items are useful for treating most health and disease problems. Remember that disasters always happen just after your local shop closes.

❏ A proprietary copper-based treatment for tackling white spot or flukes.

❏ A copper testing kit to monitor the use of the above.

❏ A disinfectant/bactericide to treat wounds or infections.

❏ Formalin in a 36% solution, obtainable from your pharmacist for treating certain flukes and some other external parasites. This has a limited shelf life, and should be replaced if a deposit occurs in the bottle.

❏ An oxygen bath, which is excellent for treating all those unrecognizable diseases not treatable with copper. This comes as a salt that you dissolve in a separate container.

effectively and fairly quickly. However, they all have one drawback - they may not be used in an aquarium containing invertebrates.

This is why it is best to start with a fish-only system. If a disease breaks out in a fish-only tank, then you can treat the whole tank immediately. If the marine system contains both fish and invertebrates, however, and one of the above diseases appears, then the only way of treating the fish is to remove them to a separate treatment tank. And since all these diseases are contagious, it often means treating all the fish from the affected tank. So, if you intend to establish a mixed fish/invertebrate system, it is vital to first establish a small, separate quarantine tank in which you can hold all newly purchased fish for a week or two in order to quarantine them and to treat any fish that do become affected.

Below: This panel summarizes just a few of the diseases that may affect marine fishes in the aquarium. If you are unsure about the problem or the possible cure, be sure to seek expert advice. And remember that an ounce of prevention is worth a ton of cure!

Above: Yellow-tail blue damselfishes (Chrysiptera parasema) *show off their brilliant colors against a background of corals and gorgonarians. Treating the fish in this aquarium would mean isolating them from the invertebrates.*

Left: This particularly nasty-looking lesion affecting this angelfish may be caused by furunculosis, considered to be the result of a bacterial infection. There are many possible health problems that marine fishes can fall prey to but a cure is not always possible in every case.

Some diseases that may affect tropical marine fishes

Marine white spot
White spot in marine fishes is caused by the single-celled parasite *Cryptocaryon irritans* and can be recognized by the appearance of small, pinhead-sized white spots, quite regular and round, evenly distributed over the body. If left untreated, the spots increase in number, until after about two weeks the fish will become distressed and die. White spot is very contagious - but not as quickly as other diseases - and can be slow to respond to treatment. The life cycle of the parasite involves the release of hundreds of free-swimming spores from cysts that fall to the aquarium floor.

Coral fish disease
Coral fish disease, caused by the single-celled parasite *Amyloodinium*, also produces spots, but they are far smaller, giving a dusted velvety appearance. ('Velvet' in freshwater fish is caused by the related parasite

Oodinium.) Often the spots can only be seen at a certain angle. About 48 hours or so after developing the disease, the affected fish invariably develops a high gill rate. If the fish is not treated very soon after this stage, death will follow, not only to the original fish, but also to all the fish in the aquarium. Your aquarium dealer will be able to supply suitable antiparasite remedies for treating both marine white spot and coral fish disease.

Flukes
Flukes take many guises, and are often difficult to diagnose. The spots (i.e. the flukes adhering closely to the skin) are irregular, both in color and shape, often being off-white and smudgy. They are just as likely to be on the fins rather than on the body. The number of flukes can vary during different times of the day and, indeed, this variation is a good indicator that flukes are present.

Flukes can be very debilitating, often marked by frequent scratching by the affected fish.

'Black flukes' are also not unusual, especially on yellow tangs, and occasionally on other yellow fish or on other tangs. Black flukes do not respond to copper medications, and need to be treated in a formalin bath. Seek expert advice about this. Once completed, transfer the fish to a new tank for two weeks, not the original, otherwise the flukes may reappear and you will need to treat the fish again.

Lymphocystis
The virus disease lymphocystis is the only other marine disease that is fairly easy to recognize and at least partly curable. The disease usually occurs on flat-sided fish, often angels, and looks like fluffy white growths on the sides of the body and fins. Improve aquarium conditions and/or add a suitable aquarium disinfectant.

Pacific longnosed butterflyfish (Forcipiger longirostris)

MARINE FISHES FOR YOUR AQUARIUM

In simple terms, there are two sorts of fish: those that live in fresh water and those that live in salt water. There are also a few species that cross the dividing line and can move from one environment to the other - salmon are a common example. Fishes are also described as 'tropical' or 'coldwater', but there is not necessarily a clear-cut division here, as there are many species that can withstand a wide range of temperature zones, and in many parts of the world - in the Mediterranean, for example - the temperature is intermediate. The important thing to remember is that the species described and discussed in this final section of the book are all tropical marine fishes, and nearly all are found on or around the world's tropical reefs - in the Indian Ocean, in the Pacific or in and around the Caribbean.

Many fishkeepers have happily kept tropical freshwater fishes for many years before deciding one day to move on to marines. Perhaps it is the sight of a clown anemonefish darting among the tentacles of an anemone that sparks their interest, perhaps it is the brilliance of the colors and patterns of marine fishes, or maybe it is the challenge of keeping these beautiful species in a carefully monitored environment that makes the prospect so exciting. Whatever the reason, marine fishkeeping has increased enormously in popularity in recent years. On the following pages you will find examples of many of the commonly available species, along with more unusual varieties and some to avoid. Perhaps you, too, will decide that you are 'hooked' by marines!

Damselfishes

Damsels are found worldwide around the tropical reefs, living in shallow waters and rarely exceeding 3in in length. Scientists call them filter-feeders, but in an aquarium they readily take solids, including flaked foods. They have many advantages for the home aquarist: they are some of the cheapest available fish, they are exceedingly hardy and disease-resistant, they are nitrite-tolerant, and very easy to feed. Many are boldly colored, and they do not grow too large for any but the smallest aquarium. They can be housed safely with many types of fish and with most invertebrates, and they can be bought singly or in small shoals.

However, there is always a catch; damsels are related to freshwater cichlids and tend to share that family's aggressive behavior. As damsels are so robust and adventurous themselves, they seem to expect other fish to share the same instincts, and many more shy and sensitive fish lose out in the competition for food and space.

Right: The yellow-tail blue damsel (Chrysiptera parasema) *is one of the smallest damsels, rarely exceeding 1.6in in the aquarium, and can be safely mixed with the most delicate companions. It can be kept singly or in a shoal, and is one of the unsung favorites of the marine hobbyist.*

Hints and tips

❑ Do not keep the larger damsel species with butterflyfishes and cowfish or any fish with trailing appendages likely to be nipped.

❑ The damsel family is hermaphrodite by nature. Put ten of these fish together, and you will identify one dominant male and nine females. Remove the male and soon one of the females will take over the male role and coloring!

Left: *Probably the most popular of the damsels is the three-spotted damselfish (Dascyllus trimaculatus). It is usually about 1in long when you buy it and grows to 2in or so in the aquarium. Young species sometimes seem to have an identity problem, behaving like cleaner wrasse at one moment and 'cleaning' other fish, and then frightening their owners by diving into anemones with the clown anemonefishes. Dominos are not as aggressive as some other damsels.*

Right: *The very untypical and shy green chromis (Chromis viridis) is a small gentle species, with subtle rather than bold coloring. It is perfect for an invertebrate set-up, but always keep it in a shoal of its own species.*

Other damsels of interest

Most damsels fit the general description, being boldly colored, very fit and active, growing to 2-3in and best kept singly or in shoals. The most popular species in this category include the neon, or black velvet damsel (*Neoglyphidodon oxyodon*), the gold-striped chromis (*Neoglyphidodon nigroris*), and the blue-fin pink damsel (*Neoglyphidodon melas*). All three have spectacular juvenile markings, but grow dull when adult. The three-striped damselfish (*Dascyllus aruanus*), the black-tailed humbug (*Dascyllus melanurus*) and the cloudy, or white-tailed, damselfish (*Dascyllus carneus*) are also popular marine subjects.

Anemonefishes

Anemonefishes, or clown anemonefishes, are not as widespread as damsels. The 30 or so species are distributed throughout the Pacific Basin, but none are native to the Caribbean area. Without exception, anemonefishes are usually good-natured towards other species, and make ideal companions in fish and in mixed fish and invertebrate systems. Unfortunately, they are not so tolerant of each other; not only is it hazardous to mix two different species, but sometimes it proves difficult to keep two members of the same species together. Anemonefishes are easy to feed, accepting any of the proprietary foods, and are reasonably hardy and disease-resistant, although they are not nitrite-tolerant. All anemonefishes enjoy what is called a symbiotic relationship with certain species of anemones. Anemones have stinging cells in their tentacles with which they stun their food - and most fish are a potential meal. Somehow, anemonefishes are immune to the stings and use the anemones for shelter and, at least to human eyes, for comfort. Their continual lazing and rubbing and general enjoyment of the anemone's charms always appears very sensual. In the wild, a number of anemonefishes often share one anemone, but this is not practical in a tank - the usual limit is two fish of the same species.

Right: Anemonefishes can be described in three convenient groups. One - the chocolate, or sebae, anemonefishes includes Amphiprion clarkii (shown here), A. bicinctus and A. sebae. Exact identification is often difficult, since each of these fish has different regional varieties. A. clarkii, for instance, can vary from a golden brown color to almost black. The chocolate anemonefishes grow to 2-3in long, are very friendly and ideal inhabitants in virtually any marine set-up.

Other anemonefishes of interest

Another group of anemonefishes includes the skunk-striped anemonefish *(A. akallopisos)* and the teak anemonefish *(A. nigripes)*. In many ways, this group is the exception that proves the rule; these small, timid fish do need an anemone in order to thrive and they do seem to prefer to live in a shoal, as opposed to being alone or one of a pair. Because of their small size, their demanding needs, and their lack of obvious color, they are the least popular of the anemonefishes for marine tanks. The spine-cheeked, or maroon, anemonefish *(Premnas biaculeatus)* is quite rare. It must be kept in a tank with no other anemonefishes, and it grows to about 3in. Because of its rarity, any imported specimens are usually snapped up quickly and they prove rewarding and long-lived aquarium subjects.

Below: In the most popular group of clown anemonefishes are the bright red forms, usually called 'red', 'tomato' or 'fire' anemone fish. These include the saddle anemonefish, Amphiprion ephippium *(pictured here), the red clown anemonefish, A. frenatus, and A. rubrocinctus. All have different markings as juveniles and regional variations. Most of the red clown anemonefishes have a white vertical stripe just behind their eyes, and many also have a dark blotch on their flanks. Red clown anemonefishes are one of the few truly red marine fish available and are popular just for the sake of variety. They grow to 2-3in in captivity and are a little more boisterous than most other clown anemonefishes. A matched pair will often live together for many years.*

Hints and tips

❏ Clown anemonefishes are bad travelers and as many of them do not survive the immigration flight, demand for these species often exceeds availability.

❏ Most clown anemonefishes do seem to survive perfectly adequately without anemones and it seems reasonably certain that it is not cruel to keep them apart. However, there is no doubt that if you cannot enjoy observing this relationship then you are missing one of the major joys of marine fishkeeping.

Left: The vivacious common clown anemonefish (Amphiprion percula or A. ocellaris) *is brilliantly colored, has a delightful temperament and rarely* exceeds 2in in captivity. The sight of one or two of these fish darting in and out of an anemone has prompted many fishkeepers to set up a marine tank.

Angelfishes

With their spectacular markings and regal bearing, angelfishes remain the undisputed 'kings' of the home aquarium. However, there is little doubt that angels as a family are a little more demanding than damsels and clown anemonefishes, so if you are a novice aquarist you should graduate to these fish and gain a few months general experience before attempting to keep this group.

Angels are reasonably hardy and robust and generally easy to feed, but they do demand high water quality. Regular water changes are essential, as angels react adversely to positive nitrate readings and a pH level that is too low (i.e. too acidic). Angels are omnivores and their diet must include vegetable matter. Since they are natural grazers and nibblers, it is important to house angels in tanks containing a sufficient layer of natural algae - just adding green food to their daily feeds is not enough. In practice, this means that angels should only be housed in aquariums with lighting sufficiently powerful to create the necessary growth of algae.

With the exception of the *Centropyge* angelfishes, which are all 'dwarf' types that rarely exceed 3in in length, most angelfishes grow to about 12-18in in the wild, and often to well over 6in in captivity. This large size, coupled with a generally peaceful nature, ensures their continuing popularity. Except among themselves, angelfishes rarely cause compatibility problems and are ideal mixers with other fish. Most angelfishes are also suitable to some extent in invertebrate tanks. Other than sponges, there are very few invertebrates that angelfishes would directly harm, so it is only their size that could cause a problem in an invertebrate tank.

Angels are quite unusual in the marine world, in that many of the larger species have two completely different color patterns during their lifetime. The two main Caribbean angelfishes, for instance - the French angel and the queen angel - are totally different as juveniles compared to their adult phase. Another feature of many of the Indo-Pacific species of angelfish, normally so distinct from each other when adult, is that they are very similarly marked when young. Thus, juvenile versions of the emperor angel, the majestic, the Koran and many more, are all navy blue with a thin white pattern, and just sufficiently different to be able to distinguish the species.

As a very general rule, do not try to mix two angels of the same size and color. For example, never mix two angels of the same type together, unless one is a juvenile and one is adult, and do not mix a juvenile emperor with a juvenile Koran. It is usually possible to find three or four sufficiently different dwarf varieties to intermix, and any dwarf will live with any larger variety.

Above: At least five or six of the dwarf angels are both beautiful and reasonably plentiful and, since they do not exceed 3in in length, extremely popular. The best-known dwarf, shown above, is probably Centropyge bispinosus, also called the coral beauty, purple angelfish, dusky angel, or red-and-blue angelfish. It is plentiful and also seems to be the hardiest. The rusty angel (Centropyge ferrugatus) and the russet angel (C. potteri) are similar in appearance, but neither is as popular nor as common as C. bispinosus, although they make useful additions to any set-up. All three angels are beautiful, but bearing compatibility in mind, it is inadvisable to house any two of them together. The flame angelfish (C. loriculus) is the most spectacularly marked of the dwarfs, its base color being a vivid red, but it is also one of the more expensive fish.

Hints and tips

❏ Angelfishes make very obvious show fish in virtually any type of marine aquarium, but only keep them if you are committed to high water quality.

❏ Dwarf angels are perfect cohabitants with any invertebrates, and in larger invertebrate tanks it is quite in order to introduce juvenile specimens of the larger angels.

❏ Adult angels want a nice quiet life. As long as any newcomer to the aquarium is not considered a threat, i.e. is quite different in looks and requirements, there should be no problem.

Below: The other popular angel from the Western Atlantic is the queen angel (Holacanthus ciliaris), a gorgeous fish in all its color phases. As with the French angel, the juveniles sometimes act as parasite cleaners for other fish.

Left: In most cases, the adult coloration outshines that of the juvenile, but with the French angel (Pomacanthus paru) from the Caribbean, most aquarists prefer the dramatic yellow and black pattern of the youngsters. Small specimens measuring 2-3in long are most often seen. The blue ring angel (P. annularis) and the Koran angel, or blue Koran, (P. semicirculatus) are among the cheapest of the available angels, especially as juveniles, and are often the first angels bought by beginners to marine fishkeeping. As they are both very hardy, this often works out well.

Above: The most popular of the angels is the emperor angel (Pomacanthus imperator), a magnificent creature that can reach about 10in in captivity. It can become as tame as the majestic, or blue-girdled, angelfish (Euxiphipops navarchus) and will also live for many years. Now that aquarists are becoming more knowledgeable and marine literature is so advanced, aquarists are no longer frightened to buy juvenile angels - it is easy to distinguish between a juvenile emperor and the juvenile blue Koran, which has similar markings but is much less expensive.

Butterflyfishes

Marine butterflyfishes are closely related to marine angels, but are quite different in appearance and in habits. Butterflyfishes are very widespread throughout the world's tropical seas wherever there are coral reefs. They rely heavily on the reefs for food, as well as for protection, and would not normally stray even a few feet away from their natural home. Butterflyfishes have a small mouth and need to peck at food constantly; consequently they are slow growers, rarely exceeding 6in long. Butterflyfishes are not fast swimmers and have no natural protection against predators other than camouflage. Therefore, not surprisingly, they are shy and rather sensitive fish. Never put butterflyfishes with boisterous fish, such as damsels and triggers, as they cannot compete either for territory or for food.

Translating the butterflyfish's natural lifestyle into a captive environment requires careful consideration. Firstly, with only two exceptions, butterflyfishes are unsuitable for invertebrate systems, since they readily attack and eat coral heads, anemones, tubeworms, cucumbers, etc. Since keeping them in a home aquarium denies these fish their natural foodstuffs, it is vital to take note of their dietary requirements and to provide them with frequent small

Below: The sunburst butterflyfish (Chaetodon kleinii) *is the easiest of the butterflyfish species to keep in the marine aquarium. Once settled in, it is hardy, it will readily accept flake food and it never seems to become involved in territorial disputes with other tank occupants. It grows to about 4in.*

meals. Since they cannot consume much food at one meal, the only chance of keeping them alive for a reasonable time is to provide frequent 'snacks'. To compound the feeding problem, many butterflyfishes will not touch flaked food, so frozen or preserved *Mysis* shrimps or brineshrimp (*Artemia salina*) are essential.

It is clear that keeping butterflyfishes presents the fishkeeper with quite a few problems. However, on the plus side, butterflyfishes will not attack other fish, they can be kept singly or in groups of any size and constituency, they are not prone to disease and are often relatively inexpensive. They grow very slowly in captivity, so they rarely cause problems of outgrowing their allotted aquarium.

Left: Every rule has its exceptions and there are some butterflyfishes that can be kept with invertebrates. The two best-known species are the copperband butterflyfish (Chelmon rostratus) pictured here and the Pacific longnosed butterflyfish (Forcipiger flavissimus). Both species have long snouts, which are adapted for eating small crustaceans from between the coral polyps. Although generally considered as coral eaters, they do not usually harm invertebrates, and do well in an invertebrate set-up. However, it is best not to keep these fish with their own kind. Both need plentiful feeds and are less shy than most other butterflyfishes.

Right: The four-eyed butterflyfish (Chaetodon capistratus) is the most common butterflyfish in the West Indies. It is relatively hardy but will not accept flake food in its diet.

Below: We should not omit to mention the spectacularly shaped poor man's Moorish idol, or pennant butterflyfish (Heniochus acuminatus). Large shoals of this fish are often seen in wildlife films, but they adapt well to aquarium life and are relatively easy feeders. They grow to about 6in in the aquarium, and live longer than many butterflyfishes. When young, they often acts as parasite cleaners for other fishes.

Below: The threadfin butterflyfish (Chaetodon auriga) is another plentiful butterflyfish found throughout the Indo-Pacific. It grows to 9in in the wild but only half this size in a tank. It makes a good, hardy aquarium inhabitant and enjoys a varied diet but, unfortunately, will not take flake food.

Tangs and surgeons

The first question to answer is what is the difference between a surgeonfish and a tang? Well, the answer is that there is no difference; some of the fish in the group are generally known as tangs, such as the yellow tang, while others are known as surgeons, such as the clown surgeon, and a few are known by both names, e.g. the achilles tang or achilles surgeon. Here, we use both names, with no biological difference intended.

Surgeons are so-called because of their 'scalpels', the two sharp bony points on either side of the body at the base of the tailfin.

Left: One group of tangs are described as sailfins, namely the yellow tang (Zebrasoma flavescens) *shown here, the brown tang* (Z. scopas) *and the striped sailfin tang* (Z. veliferum). *They are all personalities in their own right, but because of its bright single color, the yellow tang is one of the most popular marine fish. A blue surgeon and a yellow tang together provide a startling contrast. Sailfin tangs need green food even more than other tangs and surgeons; even a few days without algae can cause them to become thin and emaciated, showing the outline of their rib cage. Sailfins rarely exceed 4in and make ideal community fish.*

The scalpels can give a nasty cut to a clumsy human, but are very rarely used on other fish. Perhaps being wise to the dangers, other fish are not stupid enough to tangle with the surgeons or indeed with the tangs, which also have these weapons.

Tangs and surgeons are magnificent fish, sporting the boldest and brightest markings. They are a good size, they grow steadily, they are relatively hardy, they cause very few problems with other fish and they are easy to feed. They are safe with tiny and large fish alike, and they are ideal inhabitants for an invertebrate tank.

Tangs present only two problems. Firstly, it is absolutely essential that they are given plenty of green matter in their diet. Therefore, they should only be housed in an aquarium with plenty of light and a guaranteed supply of green algae covering the rocks on which they can nibble. However, it is not a good idea to house them in tanks in which you wish to cultivate macro algae, such as *Caulerpa*, since they will tear this to shreds as a matter of course.

Secondly, although tangs and surgeons can be mixed with virtually any other marine fish, they do cause problems among themselves. As a firm rule, you should never try and keep two of the same type together, with the one exception of the blue surgeonfish, which does not seem to mind in what number it is kept. Generally speaking, it is safer not to attempt to keep more than one fish of each genus. But, as with many marine species, it is usually in order to house a small shoal of six or more of a kind together.

Above: The best-known surgeonfish is the blue surgeonfish (Paracanthurus hepatus), *once described as the bluest thing on earth. This is a truly gorgeous fish that rarely grows to more than 3-4in in an aquarium. It is a good* feeder, and mixes with anything. Once you have progressed beyond the damsel and clown anemonefish stage, this is one of the safest marine fish to try, but always remember to provide it with adequate vegetable matter in the diet.

Below: There are a large number of surgeonfishes in the Acanthurus group. The best-known is the appropriately named powder blue surgeon (A. leucosternon), *a popular and frequently seen fish that will grow to a length of 6in in a tank. Others include the gorgeous, but rarely seen, goldrim, or Philippine, surgeonfish (A. glaucopareius),* the fairly rare and disease-prone Achilles, or red-tailed surgeon (A. achilles) *and the equally rare and even more exotically marked majestic, or striped, surgeonfish (A. bleekeri).* More often seen is the clown surgeon (A. lineatus), *which seems to thrive best in groups of its own kind. However, the rarest of all is probably the emperor tang (A. chrysurus) another beautiful surgeon that looks as though it should be a Zebrasoma. All are usually bought at 3-4in and rarely grow to more than 6-7in in captivity.*

Right: Naso lituratus, *the Japanese tang, or smoothhead, unicornfish, looks like a color variation of the powder blue surgeon. It has an affable temperament and makes an ideal if unspectacular beginner's fish. It grows to about 8in.*

Wrasses

The wrasse family is far more difficult to encompass in a general paragraph than other families. Some of the wrasses grow to only 2-3in, whereas others grow to 24in; some are ideal in an invertebrate system, others would destroy the same set-up; some need to bury at nights, some need a cave, others require neither. So really the only way to examine the wrasses in a balanced way is to describe examples of each of the most popular groups.

Right: Among the 'buriers' are the clown, or red, wrasse (Coris gaimardi) and the African clown wrasse (Coris formosa) pictured here. Both these fish are a spectacular bright red as juveniles, similar but distinguishable, and make ideal fish for the invertebrate aquarium. However, both these wrasses will grow to considerable sizes, often reaching 12in or more, during which time they completely change their coloration. The adults are far more 'sensibly' colored, and at their full-grown size are only suitable for largish fish-only systems. A closely related fish is the rarer twin-spot wrasse (Coris angulata), which starts off a beautiful silver gray color and also grows amazingly rapidly. These species are among the easiest to grow from juveniles to adults in the aquarium, enabling you to observe at first hand the spectacular color changes that take place as the fish develop.

Above: Hogfish are closely related to the wrasses. There are half a dozen or so of this subspecies, and two or three of them are quite commonly seen. The Cuban, or spotted, hogfish (Bodianus pulchellus) is imported either at about 2in in its juvenile polkadot markings or, more often, as a 6in adult. This species is usually quite inexpensive. Although hogfish are suitable companions for virtually any other fish, they will soon mess up an invertebrate system in the same way as larger wrasse. The Spanish hogfish (Bodianus rufus) has a similar juvenile pattern, but the adult (shown above) is clearly different. Probably the best-colored hogfish is the fairly rare lyretail hogfish (B. anthiodes).

Right: Many aquarists' first encounter with a wrasse is with the cleaner wrasse (Labroides dimidiatus), a thin blue-and-white fish that grows to about 3in in length. It reacts unfavorably to chemical treatments and is not very long-lived, but because of its usefulness in cleaning parasites off other tank inhabitants, many aquarists consider it an essential addition. The cleaner wrasse is an easy feeder and can be housed with virtually any invertebrate or any other fish, however large, since it enjoys the fishy equivalent of 'diplomatic immunity'. It is always worth providing this fish with a conch or a piece of coral with plenty of cavities into which it can retreat at night.

Below: The banana wrasse, another small, thin wrasse, is also an ideal inhabitant in an invertebrate set-up. Most books seem to ignore this very popular, solid yellow fish, probably because it is not easily classified. In fact, it is the juvenile version of the bluehead wrasse (Thalassoma bifasciatum), which is usually seen at 4-5in. The lyretail wrasse (T. lunare) is similar to the bluehead wrasse, but maybe not so well marked. However, it is cheap, very hardy and, like most wrasses, easy to feed. The lyretail and the banana wrasse both like to bury themselves in the sand each night. Remember when you first buy one that the fish will probably still be on Indonesian or Sri Lankan time, and will bury itself at an odd time of the day. It can take perhaps two or three months in captivity before the fish adjusts and starts to bury itself at a more 'sensible' hour, say 10.00 pm.

Left: Another marine favorite is the bird wrasse (Gomphosus coeruleus), a non-aggressive but active fish. While the female is a brown, drab, unspectacular 4in fish with a small snout, the male is a 6-7in bottle green, dolphin-shaped beauty - the star character in any large tank. But the truly amazing feature of these fish is that they are hermaphrodite, just like the blue damsels described on page 98, and it is quite possible to observe the drab, uninteresting females transform themselves in a matter of a few days.

Triggerfishes, filefishes and lionfishes

Triggerfishes

The triggerfish family is fairly small but quite widespread, one species even finding its way as far north as the English Channel. They are so-called on account of a locking spine at the front of the dorsal fin, which the fish uses to wedge itself into caves and openings. Triggers can be bought at any size from 1-9in and their hardiness and nitrite tolerance make them suitable fish for beginners, but choose their companions with care. All the triggers grow to a large size, both in the wild and in captivity, and the family has a reputation for meanness and aggressive behavior, which is not altogether unfounded. In the wild, triggers eat crustaceans, sea urchins, etc., so obviously they are the last fish to put in an invertebrate tank, but feeding them in captivity presents no problem, as they will eat anything with their strong, sharp teeth - including your fingers if you are not careful!

Above: Probably the most commonly seen trigger is the Picasso trigger, (Rhinecanthus aculeatus), not as spectacular as the others, but with just as much personality and far cheaper. The Hawaiian name for this fish is humu-humu-nuku-nuku-apuaa! There are three or four similar triggers, all suitable for the home aquarium. The best-known trigger is the clown trigger (Balistoides conspicillum). Tiny specimens are not easily caught and the fish are usually seen at 5-6in. The clown trigger is ideal for a show tank holding a few large specimen fish.

Other triggers of interest

There are a few comparatively peaceful species that, although not suitable for an invertebrate aquarium, would normally fit in with smaller fish. The best-known is the black trigger (Odonus niger), a fish with a lovely swimming action; the pink-tailed trigger (Melichthys vidua) and the white-tailed trigger (Sufflamen chrysoptera).

Filefishes

The filefishes are very closely related to triggers and often included in the same family but, superficially at least, they are quite different. Filefishes are not particularly hardy, they are not nitrite tolerant, they do not have a hard trigger, their scales are completely different, they grow very slowly in captivity, they are shy, retiring fish and they are not very easy to feed. In that they are peaceful, they do make good aquarium fish, but they have small mouths and do not eat vegetable matter, so they need feeding little and often.

Right: Most filefishes are quite drably, although not uninterestingly, colored, but the one major exception is the orange-spotted, or long-nosed, filefish (Oxymonocanthus longirostris), which is thinner than the others, far better marked, and the only filefish that lives on the reef in the wild. This fish would make an ideal companion for seahorses and razorfishes, but would demand extra loving care from its owner for long-term survival. However, its coloring and character would make this special attention worthwhile.

Lionfishes

Lionfishes, turkeyfishes, scorpionfishes, butterfly cod, call them what you will, these fish are very poisonous to humans and must be handled with care or, more accurately, not handled at all. The first seven spines of the dorsal fin carry an extremely toxic poison - verging on lethal - and only a foolhardy aquarist would try to touch the eighth spine. Bearing this warning in mind, lionfishes are very hardy and nitrite-tolerant, long-lived, slow-moving and quite good aquarium fish. The lionfish rarely attacks other aquarium fish, as long as these will not fit readily into its open mouth, and it only uses its spines in defense, whether against human or fishy predators. Do not put lionfishes with mobile invertebrates, which form their staple diet in the wild. Sometimes they are difficult to feed in captivity. In the wild, they gorge themselves periodically, so once imported they have to be weaned away from live foods and onto frozen lancefish and similar foods. In the wild they 'hang' under ledges, and are happier if given similar protection in an aquarium.

Left: The best-known lionfish is Pterois volitans, usually seen at 4-6in. Its finnage is longer than that of other lionfish. Incidentally, lionfish generally, and this species in particular, appear not to respect the immunity of cleaner wrasse, and are the cause of many unexplained disappearances of this innocuous wrasse. Quite a few other species of lionfish are offered for sale, mostly a little smaller and redder than P. volitans. Two species, Pterois antennata, the spotfin lionfish and P. sphex, the Hawaiian lionfish, are both quite popular, as is the whitefin lionfish (Pterois radiata). There are also two types of dwarf lionfishes that rarely grow to more than 3-4in in captivity, Dendrochirus zebra, the zebra lionfish and Dendrochirus brachypterus.

Groupers, sweetlips and parrotfishes

Right: The grouper family also contains many subgroups of closely related fish, some of which are worth a mention. The basslets, or 'dwarf groupers,' include the well-known royal gramma, or fairy basslet, (Gramma loreto) shown here, one of the most dramatically colored fish of all. This fish must be kept singly, but its small size allows it to be put with almost any other types of fish, and even with most invertebrates. The royal gramma rarely exceeds a length of 3in, as does the dotty-back (Pseudochromis paccagnellae), a similarly marked fish.

Other groupers of interest

The leopard, or polkadot, grouper *(Chromileptis altivelis)* is suitable for a tank containing triggerfishes and lionfishes. It is a little less solitary than other groupers. Another untypical grouper is the mimic roundhead *(Calloplesiops altivelis)*, a beautifully marked, slow-growing midwater swimmer.

Groupers and snappers

Groupers are another of those misnamed fish, since in the wild they live completely alone, one per cave - the original hermit! In an aquarium, you should not attempt to keep two of the same species together, and it is also unwise to try and keep two of any sort of groupers together. They are exceedingly hardy, nitrite-tolerant, easy to feed and disease-resistant. The grouper likes to lurk at the cave entrance, just darting out occasionally to warn off intruders or to grab a passing meal. Feed this carnivorous fish on solid chunks of food, such as mussel meat and lancefish, and make sure that its tankmates are larger than the grouper's mouth. Furnish the aquarium with an overhang large enough to accommodate your chosen fish. Groupers grow quite rapidly - in the tropics they are regarded as a prime food fish.

Closely related to the groupers are the snappers, another very large food fish. Snappers are shoaling fish that swim very powerfully and with great agility, making them difficult to catch, even in a tank. They are very hardy, nitrite-tolerant and easy to feed. Snappers grow extremely quickly and are capable of doubling their size in a matter of weeks. They are not particularly aggressive, but their very size precludes them from the average home aquarium.

Right: The emperor snapper (Lutjanus sebae) is often offered for sale at a few inches long, and its cheapness and bright markings must tempt many a beginner. However, it soon outgrows its tank, if it does not first end up as a meal for other aquarium inhabitants. In the wild it can grow to 36in long and, although generally peaceful, it is really only suitable for a public aquarium.

Sweetlips

These families are a strange hotchpotch of fish, closely related to the snappers, but different in many ways. Many members of the family grow to about 24in in the wild, but they are not regarded as food fish. In the aquarium they are far slower to adapt to captivity than other species, and very slow growers. Their natural diet consists of tiny crustaceans - they require huge amounts of these in order to thrive, and it is very difficult for the home aquarist to provide this diet. Live and meaty foods may prove viable alternatives.

Left: Easily the most popular of the sweetlips is the clown sweetlips (Gaterin chaetodonoides formerly Plectorhynchus chaetodonoides). This fish has gorgeous clownlike markings and most hobbyists would find it an almost irresistible buy. Unfortunately, these fish just do not survive in captivity. The painted *sweetlips (Spilotichthys pictus) - a beautiful yellow-and-black, horizontally striped juvenile fish, but a dull and boring adult - and the oriental sweetlips shown left (Gaterin orientalis formerly Plectorhynchus orientalis) are both more adaptable to life in an aquarium.*

Parrotfishes

Parrotfish are wrasselike fish that normally grow many feet long in the wild. Their natural diet consists of coral heads, so they are only suitable for certain aquariums. There are many species in the wild, and indeed quite a few are offered for sale, but often they are not identified. They mix well with wrasses and groupers.

Above: The attractive red-and-white bicolor parrotfish (Bolbometopon bicolor) fits into any largish fish-only set up. This is another marine fish in which the adult markings are totally different to those of the juveniles.

Boxfishes, pufferfishes and hawkfishes

Left: Among the boxfishes, the cowfish (Lactoria cornuta), so-called because of its 'horns,' is typical of the group, as is the similar camel, or pyramid, trunkfish (Tetrasoma gibbosus). Both of these are 'character' fish, and ideal in an invertebrate aquarium. They can be hand fed, and neither give off a poison in the tank. Ideally, keep these types of fish in an aquarium with living rock, where they can peck and graze all day without waiting for 'feeding time'.

Below: The boxfish (Ostracion cubicus) shown here is a little beauty that starts out looking like a tiny dice - perhaps as small as 0.15in³ - very pale yellow with black dots. As it grows, the body elongates and the patterning changes dramatically, turning dark mustard with blue spots. Equally striking is the spotted boxfish (Ostracion meleagris). It is one of the few easily sexable species. Both sexes have a dark body with white spots, but the male's patterns are far more vivid, with additional tints of blue on the fins. A pair of these gorgeous fishes is a fine acquisition, but only rarely seen.

Boxfishes

Some of the boxfishes, or trunkfishes, are so cute that they simply cannot be ignored. These fish are cube or cuboid in shape, and have a hard exterior (though not an ectoskeleton). The hardened skin is only softer around the eyes, mouth and fins, so these fish swim as though in a straitjacket. They are very slow swimmers, though quite maneuverable, and settle down well to aquarium life, although they are obviously not adept at battling for food. Smaller species fit well into invertebrate systems. One word of caution - many boxfishes species give off a poison if severely threatened. This does not occur very regularly, but in the confines of an aquarium the result is invariably a total wipe-out, so choose their companions carefully.

Pufferfishes

Just like boxfishes, puffers have an awkward, unfishlike shape and use their fins, rather than their bodies, for forward motion. But instead of a hard casing of scales, puffers have the most soft and pliable skin, which allows the fish to inflate itself many times greater than its original size in times of danger. Puffers can do this in or out of water, using water or air. Although they do not give off a poison, many of them have poisonous flesh, so marine and human predators must exercise caution when eating them. Puffers are good aquarium fishes - they are hardy, have strong personalities and are disease-resistant. They rarely cause problems with other fish and eat almost anything. In fact, they are often quite greedy and sometimes tear food away from other fish. The puffers' natural diet includes many small crustaceans, mollusks and urchins, which they attack with their strong 'beak', so they are not suitable for a mixed invertebrate aquarium, although they would not harm corals or anemones.

Right: The porcupinefish (Diodon hystrix) is covered with sharp spines but is suitable for most set-ups. Many varieties of the sharpnosed puffer (Canthigaster sp.) are considerably smaller, but also make good general fish. The very beautiful black-spotted puffer (Arothron nigropunctatus) is normally seen at 4-5in but grows to about double this size. The white-spotted puffer (A. meleagris) and the reticulated blowfish (A. reticularis) only differ in their markings.

Below: The most spectacular hawkfish is the longnosed hawkfish (Oxycirrhites typus), which can be housed safely with virtually anything, except shrimps. Its comparative rarity means it is quite expensive. The spotted hawkfish (Cirrhitichthys aprinus) is more reasonably priced and probably embodies the ideal typical beginners' fish better than any other.

Hawkfishes

Hawkfishes are smallish predators that readily adapt to aquarium life. Most species rarely grow more than 3-4in, so as long as they are not housed with tiny fish or smallish shrimps, they can be put with most other available animals. Hawkfishes spend most of their time perched on rocks and ledges watching the world go by - they are not 'dozy' like lionfishes, for instance, but alert and upright, even though they are stationary. When something takes their interest, whether it be food or a threat, they dart off the rock in a hawklike fashion in order to investigate, hence their common name. These excellent community fish never cause problems with other aquarium inhabitants; if regularly fed they can live for many years in captivity.

Gobies, blennies and batfishes

Left: The white firefish, or spike-finned goby, (Nemateleotris magnifica) is a burrowing fish imported in large numbers. The equally popular golden-headed sleeper (Eleotrides strigatus) is a gorgeously marked fish, with more subtle coloration than most marines. It lives in a self-made tunnel in the sand, maintaining a nearly vertical position, with just its head poking out.

Below: The beautifully marked mandarin goby, or mandarinfish, (Synchiropus splendidus) is a perennial favorite but not easy to feed in captivity - it very rarely accepts dried or frozen foods, usually insisting on live brineshrimp or rotifers. For this reason, it is an ideal occupant in a tank with large clumps of living rock, but rarely survives in any other environment.

Gobies

The typical goby is a small, tube-shaped fish, perhaps 2-4in long and often drably colored. It spends most of its life scurrying along the sand. Many gobies live in small caves or among coral branches and many enjoy a symbiotic relationship with other animals, most notably with certain species of shrimps. Since most gobies are very hardy and disease-resistant and never cause compatibility problems, the small percentage of brightly colored species make excellent aquarium inhabitants. In addition, they are generally easy to feed, readily available and not expensive.

Other gobies of interest

The neon goby (*Gobiosoma oceanops*) is one of the smallest species - little larger than a match stick - but an interesting aquarium subject. It has proved willing to breed in captivity and shares the same markings as the cleaner wrasse (*Labroides dimidiatus*), fulfilling a similar function in the aquarium. These tiny fish are best kept in small shoals. The Catalina Sea off the coast of California is home to the Catalina goby (*Lythrypnus dalli*), a bright red fish of similar proportions to the neon. Its attractive color makes this fish an instant choice, but do make sure that the aquarium temperature remains in the low 70s°F if this fish is to survive.

Blennies

The blenny family is very similar to the gobies. Blennies are also generally drab, smallish, bottom-dwelling fish, and some species do not obviously fit into either family. Blennies are just as hardy as the gobies and ideal for beginners, although there are perhaps not as many varieties from which to choose as fewer are imported.

A predator in disguise

Beware of the 'false cleaner' (*Aspidontus taeniatus*), a blenny but only just distinguishable from the cleaner wrasse (*Labroides dimidiatus*). Its mouth is a different shape and it lives off the slime of unsuspecting fish, which can receive nasty bites from this evil mimic.

Below: A long-time favorite species is the entertaining bicolor blenny (Escenius pulcher), a very slimy, slithery fish, 2-3in in length. It always chooses to make its home in a small hole in the rocks, constantly darting out inquisitively and returning with equal speed. This is an aquarium fish with real personality! Another blenny offered for sale is the appropriately named zebra blenny (Meiacanthus grammistes), which reaches about 4in long.

Batfishes

As a complete contrast to the smallish fish that have been described so far, we come to the giant batfish. This fish, although often acquired at just 1-3in long, will grow prodigiously, even in an aquarium, and very soon reaches 10-12in in size, being tall rather than long. It is one of the few fish that actually outgrows its immediate environment, and many aquarists are faced with the problem of either buying another tank or part-exchanging their rapidly expanding fish. Batfishes like to 'rule' a tank by swimming unhindered in the open spaces, and as long as other fish do not challenge this right of way, batfishes are normally content to live with any other fish, from small gobies up to larger groupers and triggers. However, choosing tankmates can be a problem. Batfishes are normally bought when small and at that size they are very vulnerable and can soon end up quite battered, since their only natural protection seems to be their intimidating adult size. Obviously, batfishes will only grow if they are sufficiently well-fed - they are constantly hungry and seemingly greedy fish that eat virtually anything. Unfortunately, this includes most invertebrates, including supposedly poisonous species, such as anemones.

Left: The orbiculate batfish (Platax orbicularis) shown here starts off like an autumn leaf drifting in the current. A few months later, it is the size of a plate. The long-finned batfish (Platax tiera) is also most striking when juvenile. Its long, flowing fins seem to shorten gradually as the body develops.

117

Other varieties

Most of the fish described so far fit into neat categories and it would be fairly simple for the reader with, for example, a trigger species not mentioned in the text to determine the likely characteristics of the fish in question. But nature does not like neat packages and you will encounter many types of fish that are, say, in a family of their own or the only member of a larger family suitable for the aquarium. Here we take a brief look at some of the other species occasionally offered for sale that make interesting aquarium occupants, including the hardiest of all species suitable for a marine tank - the brackish species - and some of the most awkward subjects - the seahorses.

Below: A cousin of the tangs, the lo rabbitfish (Lo vulpinus) is a nicely marked, rather innocuous fish, not very common, but an ideal addition to an invertebrate community. Supposedly also related to tangs, the Moorish idol (Zanclus cornutus) is one of the most spectacular marine fish. It is common in the wild, but never really settles into captivity, and even apparently healthy and settled species may roll over and die without notice or apparent reason. Wildlife films often feature shoals of this species swimming over the reefs, but the home aquarist would fare better with the similarly marked poor man's Moorish idol, or pennant butterflyfish, (Heniochus acuminatus) on page 105.

Above: The freshwater aquarist will be familiar with quite a few so-called brackish fish, i.e. fish that normally inhabit river estuaries and can adapt to both fresh water and salt water, but are probably happiest in conditions that lie somewhere in between. Monodactylus argenteus, *the mono, moonfish or silver batfish, for example, is an incredibly hardy species, often used as a starter fish. It is usually bought at 1-2in long and slowly grows to 5-6in. Its brilliant silver markings make a fine display in a freshwater aquarium, although pale against the brighter colors of true marine fish. Other brackish fish include the rarer and more difficult species* Monodactylus sebae, *which will not tolerate completely fresh water, the spotted scat (Scatophagus argus) and the targetfish (Therapon jarbua).*

Seahorses in the aquarium

The problem with seahorses is that no other animal is more appealing, especially to newcomers, but few survive in captivity. Seahorses not only seem very reluctant to feed in an aquarium, they also seem accident prone, blundering into anemones, succumbing to the clutches of a hermit crab or the suction force of a power filter inlet. So, if you wish to keep seahorses, provide a tank with no dangers, virtually no competition as far as feeding is concerned and remember they need live foods every day.

Below: You may be tempted to keep a seahorse (Hippocampus sp.) but be prepared for disappointment.

Above: Various types of cardinalfish are seen in aquarium shops. The most interesting one, the red spotted, or orbiculate, cardinalfish (Sphaeramia nematoptera, formerly Apogon orbicularis) does not look like its companions. It could easily be mistaken for a freshwater variety - its colors are unusual but not dramatic; it only grows to 2in, it is a slow, peaceful swimmer, very hardy and ideal for a beginner, except that it will not eat flake foods.

Right: Over a dozen types of goatfish are imported on occasion and these peaceful scavengers spend their days rummaging through the sand. They do not grow very large, seem completely oblivious to other aquarium inhabitants and make an interesting addition to most types of marine community.

Freshwater index

Marine index

Picture credits

The photographs have been credited by page number and position on the page: (B)Bottom, (T)Top, (C)Center, (BL)Bottom left, etc.

Commissioned photography
Neil Sutherland © Colour Library Books: Endpapers, half-title page, 10, 12-13, 14-15, 16-17, 18-19, 20, 22(L), 24, 25, 28, 29(T), 32, 34, 37, 38, 39, 40-1, 42, 43(B), 44(L), 46, 48-49, 50-51, 52-53, 54(B), 55, 56(T), 57(T,B), 58, 59(T), 60-1, 63, 64, 66, 67(B), 69(TR,B), 70(C), 71, 73(B), 74(B), 79, 81, 84-85, 86-87, 88-89

Additional photographs
The publishers wish to thank the following photographers who have supplied photographs for this book.

David Allison: 21, 43(T), 72 (T,B), 80(B), 107(T), 109(BR), 118(B)

Dr. James C. Chubb: 30(B), 31

Les Holliday: 73(T), 91(TR), 92(TL, BL), 105(BL), 108(BR), 113(T), 116(T)

Ideas into Print: 26, 27, 29(B), 92(BR)

Paul Kay: Contents page (L,R), 77, 101(R), 111(B)

Alex Kerstitch: 115(B), 119(BR)

Jan-Eric Larsson: 33(B), 56(B), 82, 103(T), 115(C)

Barry Pengilley: 112-113(B), 117(B)

Max Gibbs, The Goldfish Bowl, Oxford: Title page, 22-3(C), 30(T), 36, 44-45, 47, 54(T), 59(B), 65(T,B), 67(T), 68, 69(TL), 70(B), 75(T), 78(T), 80(T), 90-91, 94-95, 96, 98(T,B), 99, 100, 10l(L), 102(T,B), 103(B), 104(T,B), 105(BR), 106(B), 107(B), 108(TL), 108-109(T), 109(BL), 110, 111(T), 112(T), 113(B), 114(T,B), 116(BR), 117(T), 118(T), 119(T,BC)

Mike Sandford: 33(T), 40(C), 57(CR), 62, 74(T), 75(B), 76, 78(B), 105(T), 106(T)

Artists
The artwork illustrations in the book have been prepared by the following artists. (Copyright is the property of Colour Library Books.)

Rod Ferring: 14, 86, 87

Glenn Smith: 12, 20, 21, 30, 93

Acknowledgments
The publishers would like to thank Heaver Tropics for their help in supplying fish foods for photography.